NEXT GENERATION LEADERSHIP SKILLS

LEARN HOW TO BE THE CHANGE YOU WISH TO SEE

Copyright © 2024 Phil Roberts

All rights reserved. No part of this book may be reproduced, stored in any retrieval system, or transmitted in any form or by any means, electronic, mechanical, photocopying, recording, or otherwise, without express written permission of the author or publisher.

The moral right of the author has been asserted.

First published in 2024

ISBN: 9798870706023

NEXT GENERATION LEADERSHIP SKILLS

LEARN HOW TO BE THE CHANGE YOU WISH TO SEE

PHIL ROBERTS

To Morgan and India. Providers of all the inspiration I will ever need.

CONTENTS

Foreword — 11

One
Who Are You — 17

Two
What Got You Here — 24

Three
Accelerate Your Growth with Self-Awareness — 37

Four
What Rumbles Underneath — 64

Five
The Rats Fighting in a Sack — 85

Six
Have You Got the Courage to be Human — 104

Seven
What Do You Stand For — 131

Eight
Cultivating Your Innate Wisdom — 153

Nine
Change Agency for the Self — 177

Ten
Integration — 199

Eleven
My Leadership Story; Why I Wrote This Book — 203

Acknowledgements — 209
About the Author — 211
Bibliography — 213

FOREWORD

Most of us spend our lives dealing with a series of professional and personal challenges of one sort or another, hopefully interspersed with moments when we are in our zone and thriving, or at least in periods of relative calm and stability. When we are faced with challenges, we don't always handle whatever is going on as well as we would like to, and find that our reactions and our responses somehow fall short of what might be expected, such that we can end up feeling bemused, confused, and even frustrated with ourselves. In these moments we know that we almost certainly could have been more effective, have achieved more, or have had a better impact on other people. We instinctively know that there is a more capable and convincing version of who we are waiting to emerge, and yet it can be hard to figure out how to go about doing this.

If, on top of all this, we are in a formal or an informal leadership role, then we will know that we automatically affect other people as we work with and through them, and find that we need to consider what other people might also find difficult and challenging. Those that we lead and are with affect us too, simply because that is the nature of being human, and if the mutual affect is anything other than easeful we have the potential for misunderstanding and triggering. It is usually the 'relational', people-parts of leadership and management that are the most difficult.

Most of us, therefore, will need to develop if we are to be successful in our work. If we wish to lead and to make some sort of difference in whatever endeavour we are involved in, we will have to learn how to do this, and a fundamental part of this learning is about our psychological and emotional identity. Everything that we do is driven by these two aspects of who we are.

Developing who we are, alongside of what we do, will enable us to build a powerful and compelling leadership identity, to say nothing of who we have the potential to become as people. By developing who we are we become clearer and cleaner within ourselves, and as we do this our impact on the people around us dramatically increases. Having some way of navigating our interior world therefore becomes crucial, a differentiator if you like, and this is what *Next Generation Leadership Skills* sets out to do.

As we consider the context for our leadership we begin to realise that there are many people and groups with a vested interest in how successful we are. When we ask the leaders of the organisations that we all rely on to stand up to be counted, whether this is in the private, public or third sector, we must have a good idea of what we expect of them. One day this might be you. It might even be you right now. We need to signpost to leaders young and old, as well as leaders-in-waiting, what the development work looks like alongside the work of business schools and universities.

Our psychological and emotional maturity are central to how we lead and follow, and to how we make decisions. It is as a result of our decisions that our (and others) lives are lived, and how the future is written. For most of us the majority of our decisions are unconscious. We all make countless decisions each day about how to communicate and to collaborate, how we weigh things up, how we react to a perceived threat, what we assume, what we believe to be true, and more. Our decisions are heavily influenced by our automatic patterns, and we unthinkingly implement them with our biases and sometimes our relational clumsiness. We are required to be both individually *and* collectively minded as we continually balance our needs with those of others. To thrive we have to be able to manage our boundaries well. Depending on our psychological and emotional profile some of these things may be difficult.

Of course, in many respects we are brilliant too, and yet we seem to be able to find ways to tarnish our brilliance such that we don't always shine as brightly as we might do.

This book is important because the decisions that we make matter. Not just for ourselves, but also for those around us and those that will inherit the legacy of what we decide. The more responsibility that we have, the bigger the impact that our decisions will have.

It is important too because the alternative to having psychologically aware and emotionally literate, wise and intuitive leaders, is to rely upon leaders that lack maturity and wisdom. None of us should want this. The quality of decisions made will be poorer as a result, diminishing us all in the process.

Furthermore, it is simply more satisfying and enriching to be working at our very best and to be reaching our full potential. As we learn how to be the change that we wish to see in the world, we will continue to work hard, yet with a lighter touch and a defter approach, knowing that as we mature our congruence and our presence is doing some of the heavy lifting for us.

Anyone that is involved in change agency can add extra horsepower to their work by learning to use who they are as a tool for change, alongside classical change management practices. We can *be* a change agent, using just our presence.

We will take a look at how our everyday lives – professional and personal – present us with what we need to learn, and the amazing insights we can take from building our self-awareness and developing a mindful attitude; perhaps the most important building blocks for change agency leadership. Then we will take a deep dive into psychological and emotional maturity, the two huge engines that drive our behaviour and what we do. Next, we will ask what it is that we stand for by defining our personal values, before asking how we can each cultivate and use our innate wisdom. We will end by acknowledging that getting change to stick can sometimes be difficult, and asking what we can do to integrate and embody what we learn.

Each chapter is summarized, and offer a series of practical exercises. There are case studies for most chapters, based on real people and situations from my coaching and consulting practice. Names and certain aspects of the context have been changed to preserve anonymity and confidentiality.

The style of writing in this book is deliberately lyrical. It is designed to appeal to the way that we feel as well as to the way that we think, because our intuition and who we are go beyond the traditional five senses. It seems obvious to me that a book about psychological and emotional maturity needs to 'walk its talk'. Nevertheless, I hope that this book is also clear, assertive where it needs to be, and offers a call to action.

If you feel like you have a fire burning deeply inside of you, waiting for the right time for it to ignite, this book will fan the embers. It can kick start a personal journey that takes you way beyond who you are now and allow you to craft your life using what you already have buried inside of you. This book is not about material success, although that may follow as a by-product of your brilliance, but about the essence of who you are and who you might become. You can become the person that others look at and instinctively choose to follow, without you making any effort. Above everything else, you can become your own person, on your own terms, fully aware of the edges and the flaws that sit alongside what you love to do and are brilliant at. There can be no finer goal in life than to become the best version of who you are.

Ultimately, *Next Generation Leadership Skills: Learn How to be the Change You Wish to See in the World* will help you to thrive, and those around you to give off their best as they work with and for you.

ONE

WHO ARE YOU?

"It is only our deeds that reveal who we are."
Carl Jung

I have the good fortune to work in many countries as a coach and a facilitator. In doing so I have accumulated experience of the many kinds of differences that exist between us, and have done my best to understand and navigate through these differences. They are real and they show up in many different ways when we set out to get stuff done together.

In parallel to my professional work I have also explored many alternative ways of thinking and being in what we might call the transpersonal space for over thirty years, and here too we encounter all kinds of differences much of the time.

In both the mainstream and the non-mainstream environments some of these differences are obvious, while many remain invisible and almost impossible to notice unless we really pay attention. Difference appears everywhere, and yet this isn't just a book about our differences. It is also about how in many important ways we are the same, all of us with our unique blend that makes us "us". We are each a living breathing paradox, completely unique individuals and yet of the same blueprint and made with the same materials as everyone else. Many of us are fortunate to be individual, sovereign people, while also being one of eight billion or so of the same species sharing the planet.

For example, most of us tend to care about the same things, like our status, our need for belonging to the groups that we are in, and our need for some level of control over our own lives. We are for the most part built the same way with a psychology and emotions, physiological systems – nervous, endocrine, and others – neuroses and ambitions, and hopes and fears. All of us need to feel some level of safety to function well, whether this need is high or low. We don't all believe the same things, however we each have belief systems that we use to greater or lesser degrees. We all have our conscious and unconscious bias. We will each express all of these things in our own particular way.

Most of us reading this will have grown into adults, or at least into some kind of physical maturity. We shall see later how we might sometimes come to remain adolescent or even child-like even when we are appearing as an adult with serious responsibilities.

We also know from studies in adult development that each and every one of us has the potential to continue developing and maturing throughout our entire lives, right up until we take our last breath. Whether we do this or not is ultimately a personal choice. Perhaps the greatest work of innovation we can ever do is to make positive choices to stretch outside of our comfort zones from time to time and to continue evolving into ever more effective and capable versions of who we are.

Our work will almost certainly require us to develop, whatever sphere of work we are involved in. This could be as we take on a new job, when we get promoted, if we are asked to lead something of which we haven't much experience, when there is crisis, or when we need to look for an uplift in what we deliver.

Whenever we take on new opportunities and responsibilities or experience hardship or something challenging, in important ways we are being asked to step into new territory. These moments may demand something of us that sometimes we are well equipped to respond to, while at other times it has a more profound feel as if we know that what is asked will require some courage and commitment. There are times in our lives and careers when we are unquestionably at a crossroads; some kind of threshold that we need to cross.

These invitations to grow, addressed to the deeper parts of who we are, can be accepted or they can be refused. No one will make a judgement about the choice that we make. From where the invitation comes who knows? Perhaps we could say that it is our souls yearning for attention and fulfilment.

If what is asked of us is significant in some way, it will usually be easier for us to take the road that we know and that feels safe and comfortable. A decision will therefore have been made to continue viewing the world and who we are in the same way. For the most part this will do, at least for now. We will muddle along for a bit longer.

Over time, if we remain on this road we might become aware of our unlived life, the inner parts of us that we haven't exercised or stretched, or expressed, and take a look around. What we see might shock us. We will see the same invitation gathering dust in some distant part of our psyche, and perhaps then we will pick it up.

The rest of this book is about what happens when we accept the invitation to grow and develop, however and whenever it has arrived, and regardless of who might have sent it.

The map that we might use to navigate our way through the territory of growth and development, if there were such a thing, would be enormous; such is the complexity of the nature of being human. It feels presumptive to even contemplate the drawing of such a map, and yet this book is also an attempt to do just that. The focus is heavily oriented towards our interior rather than the exterior, notwithstanding that the context and what is 'out there' always shapes our understanding and drives our actions. We will work with not just our conscious behaviour, but our unconscious drivers too. It is more about who we are than what we know and our technical skills.

We will see that our behaviour and what we actually decide to do is determined by what we think and what we feel about the situation we are in.

Our cognition and our emotion are in turn strongly influenced by our psychology, our physiology, and our beliefs and our assumptions. Events around us trigger a series of conscious and unconscious inner activities that show up as thoughts and feelings.

Our psychology and how our physiology works have been shaped in large part by our genetics, our biography and our significant life experiences, our education, and the culture around us when we were growing up. Whether we chose them or not our role models crept into our bones and shaped who we are. For many of us they still quietly sit there, pulling our strings.

Our ancestry too has moulded us and framed the stories we grabbed hold of as young people when we first began to imagine the lives that we might lead.

Sitting under and around all of this is our unconscious and how we make sense of our lives and everything around us. For some, this is called spirituality or mystery and thus we enter the world of mythology, dreams, and beliefs.

We can see that the map is vast and interconnected; there is much for us to work with as we figure out what and how to develop. By paying attention to our inner world, we develop our intuitive abilities, adding richness and options to our leadership identity and practice.

"To know thyself is the beginning of wisdom."
Socrates, c2400 years ago

"Who looks outside dreams; who looks inside, awakes."
Carl Jung, c2300 years later

Our dreaming is important, as is the awakening of our relationship to the deeper parts of who we are. Only then can we reach our full potential and achieve things that those who chose to stay on the safe road would find impossible to even imagine.

This book will have the flavour of leadership simply because that is my professional background. Most of us lead at times, even if this is informal, and we all have to follow from time to time. The implicit questions this book will ask are how you can lead more effectively, who it actually is that other people are being asked to follow, and even perhaps why they should bother?

Over the last fifty years there have been many truly excellent leadership development, self-help and general development books written. I have read and used many of them, and continue to go back to them and current material as a leadership developpment practitioner and eternal student of behaviour, meaning, and leadership. This book is written for anyone with similar interest.

It will go deep, and necessarily so, as what drives us and influences our behaviour and therefore our decision-making, can be well buried.

The hope and the payoff will be that as you start to answer the question, 'who are you?', that we end up living the life that we want to, and doing work that satisfies and maybe even enriches us. At a broader level my hope is that we end up with higher quality leaders; as driven, bright and capable as anyone ever has been, and yet with the higher-level capability of using themselves as the tools for change so that the decisions made benefit our wider society, and the generations to come.

"What we think, we become."

Buddha

TWO

WHAT GOT YOU HERE…

"…won't get you there."

Marshall Goldsmith

This chapter is about the importance of preparing well for what lies ahead, and of paying attention to what we need to learn from the situations that we find ourselves in. As we build our leadership capacity some of this learning will be about who we are as people. Being clear about what we need to learn will get us to where we need to be more quickly.

A year or so ago I coached an Italian lawyer who worked in France for a large multi-national as in-house General Counsel. He had just been promoted to a far larger and more complicated portfolio in the US and one of the contexts for the new role was an impenetrable matrix of formal and informal reporting lines, for which he would need a deft touch.

Gianni was highly driven, extremely bright, very

opinionated, and hugely ambitious. Like many in his profession he worked incredibly hard with punishingly long hours. This combination of characteristics had placed him on the radar of the right people, and his ability to manage his reputation with his bosses got him on to the short list and ultimately, the appointment. He had played his hand well. It was only a few weeks later however, settling into his new role and different way of life for him and his family, when he tripped up.

He was attending an informal 'getting to know you' gathering of thirty or so colleagues over lunch, and was the most senior person there. A discussion somehow began about a US public holiday that celebrated an Italian cultural hero, and which ended up with Gianni passionately defending the hero's name against accusations of imperialism and brutality. Gianni had a strong need to be right and to win an argument, any argument in fact, stemming from his professional training. Culturally too, he was used to asserting himself in forthright and very clear ways, and being respected for doing so. The lunch ended awkwardly and Gianni was confused and upset about the reaction he had.

He wondered out loud why it had been such an issue, and I asked him what he might have misunderstood and what he would have done differently if he had his time over. He found the questions difficult to answer.

In our discussions it slowly became clear for

Gianni that he had chosen lawyerly argument as his way of engaging with a relaxed and wide-ranging group of colleagues. The topic was important to his Italian identity, and he felt strongly about it. He hadn't recognised the symbolism of his role as being the most senior leader at the lunch, with all of the role modelling and relational sensitivity that this involved.

He was silent as he contemplated what the step up to a higher level of leadership responsibility actually meant for how he needed to operate. A penny in his mind started to drop. Slowly he began to engage with how he would need to adapt his approach. He realised that he would have to tone down the force of his personality and not need so much assertion of his own views. Instead he would have to ask more questions and listen well to the answers. More ears than mouth. He would also have to stop searching for the weakness in others' positions and start to build relationships based on mutual respect and win-win outcomes. Differences would need to be respected, and be seen to be respected. He learned that a defter touch would be essential.

Gianni worked out what to let go of so that he could have the impact that he wanted, and he came to realise that as he did so, his reputation looked after itself.

He had understood that what got him to the US wouldn't be enough to keep him there.

By unthinkingly sticking with the skills and attitudes that got him promoted, he endured a degree of reputational damage that required valuable energy to repair, and which would undoubtedly get in the way of him establishing himself if he didn't change tack. The experience humbled him and may even be seen to have served him; it was however avoidable and unnecessary.

This kind of story is not unusual as we win the prizes that we have worked so hard for, and they get told in many ways.

For example, as we step up to our first management role we find that we can no longer rely solely on our own abilities to do a good job. Someone else's performance will determine how successful we are. Yet, we became a manager most likely as we did a great job as an individual contributor. The very abilities that got us promoted we can no longer use! We quickly realise that what got us here almost certainly won't get us there.

The same dynamic plays out throughout our careers. Charan, Drotter and Noel captured this well in their 2003 book *The Leadership Pipeline* [1], as they defined the seven career steps that are most likely to trip us up. The first (as just described) and the last (to CEO or equivalent) are usually considered to be the hardest. The step to CEO requires a significant shift in emphasis from more internal focus on whatever the organisation is up to, to more external focus and investor and political management, M&A,

strategic alliances, stock prices, sector dynamics and the like. Plus, of course, by its very nature the position at the top is considerably exposing and for many, quite lonely. Many underestimate the steepness of this step.

Another example is of a passionate campaigner for a cause who takes on higher profile role with more positional influence. The choice becomes whether to keep throwing rocks at those they are campaigning against, or to choose a different way to engage with those who up until only recently they described as the enemy. Black and white becomes infused with shades of grey.

If our campaigner is mindful, they may be able to detach and make a conscious choice to continue rock throwing or not. If so, this becomes a strategic decision, weighed up in the round and with careful assessment of the risk and reward.

When we are developing, upgrading, growing, taking on more responsibility, we will have skills, attitudes and behaviours that will continue to serve us well, and some that are no longer required and may even hinder our future success.

Why is it so hard to let go of what we no longer need? Even though the letting go is hard, the answer is simple. We each work and train over many years to establish our professional and adult identity. We have pride in what we have done well and enjoyment in what we have to show for it. Our ego, the part of us that we construct in part to feel good about ourselves, has fed well on what has made us stand out and is seduced by the positive feedback, the accolades, and the rewards. Being asked to let go of the very things that have helped to establish our identity can be deeply troubling to our psyche. It feels like we have to relinquish a part of who we are. This can be threatening and leave us feeling vulnerable, and to some extent incapable as we begin our new work.

Surely some conscious thought about all of this will be useful? We do not, after all, wish to be the architects of our own downfall or delay the time it takes to succeed at whatever we do next.

To avoid the discomfort of confronting the work of change many of us won't even think about it. We will put our heads down, muddle through and press on even as we sense that something isn't quite right. We will gradually find ways to cope as we work out what is required, and inevitably mistakes will be made. If we are fortunate we will have support during this process, others will be patient, and the mistakes will not be terminal.

If we choose instead to set ourselves up in the best way that we can, we can begin with an honest assessment of ourselves. This will lead to the self-awareness of what we need to let go of so that we can move forward cleanly. When we do this well, we blunt the effect of our out of date behaviours so that they don't become ghosts that reappear as some behavioural echo when we least expect it.

There can be a sadness and regret at the letting go, almost as if we are saying goodbye to a loyal friend. Accountants and lawyers in big firms who follow the Partner track will now spend more time in meetings and staring at spreadsheets than in practicing accounting or law. The marketing guru is suddenly a 'Head of' or 'Chief of' and now oversees marketing. The campaigner is no longer in the boat or climbing up the side of a tower block.

This can be a real issue. We compromise what we love to do for what we think we want. The act of buying in to someone else's idea of success, be it a well-meaning boss or a family expectation, can leave us bereft in later life. We need to take care with our decisions of what we let go, lest we abandon the best parts of ourselves, the parts that shine and that make our hearts sing.

Seen from the perspective of ambition the word 'leadership' is a baited psychological trap for the unwary ego. How many really good bosses have you had? Fewer than you deserve. The well-worn cliché, 'be careful what you wish for' is tailor made for those desperate to be leaders. Those whose ambition outstrips their talent and their experience, are more likely to crash and burn as they rush headlong into their new status and avoid doing the necessary development work.

A hawk's eye view reveals the way in which our careers and our lives become repeating cycles of growth and development, and of working out what to dial up and dial down. The times of growth are punctuated with times when we plateau. These quieter times are essential, for it is then that we integrate and learn to embody the changes that we have made. Sometimes it may feel that instead of plateauing that we are going backwards, or worse still that we have failed at something. The smart people will mine the failures for honest insight and learning, and come back stronger.

How many of us run internal operating programmes that we ought to have closed down many years ago? How often do we meet someone from the past, a friend or an ex-colleague, and ask are they *still* doing that?

On the other hand, a client I have worked with for many years clearly does his development work well. As he takes on more and more responsibility, he quickly establishes himself and after only a short amount of time has looked polished and congruent. He has evolved and matured while remaining authentic. It is inspiring to see. He has thought about what he needs to let go of as well as what he needs to learn.

The moment where we tilt from one way of thinking and seeing to another is the shift we are looking for. Gianni experienced this moment in our coaching. This outgrowing of our older mindsets is important. Who amongst us thinks about work and life the same way as when we were just starting out?

Once we have a clear-sighted perspective on our

current reality and we know what we no longer need to be or do, we can begin the nuts and bolts work of development; of goal setting, learning, trying out, adapting, reviewing, looking for feedback, and persevering. We can shed the old skin and discover our latent strengths and the skills that were there all along. With practice we then stretch and flex our new muscles, we burnish and integrate them into the expanded sense of who we are, until they become normal and we think they have always been there.

As this cycle of expansion and integration repeats throughout our lives the idea that we will somehow get 'there' and all will be well, is a fallacy. The best that we can hope for is that we become set up for the current phase before we start to think about what might be next, and the whole thing starts again. We are permanently a work in progress, what Bob Dylan talked of as a state of constantly becoming. The depth and quality of our foundations become barometers for how well we will surf the waves of ambiguity and uncertainty, as we endlessly discover and reveal to ourselves who we are.

What greater work or act of innovation can there be than to constantly become?

"When I let go of what I am, I become what I might be."
- Lao Tzu

SUMMARY

- When we take on new responsibilities we will have knowledge, skills and attitudes that will continue to serve us well, and some that are no longer required and may even hinder our future success.

- Letting go of what we did that has made us successful can be difficult.

- We can set ourselves up for future success by doing an honest assessment of ourselves.

- Once we have a clear-sighted perspective on our current reality and we know what we no longer need to be or do, we can begin the nuts and bolts work of development.

- Our careers and our lives become repeating cycles of growth and development, and plateauing. It is in these quieter phases that we integrate and embody what we have learned.

EXERCISES

With a calm detached attitude...

1. Take a good look at the next phase you are embarking on, whether it is a new job, a change of circumstance, an unexpected development, or any situation that feels as if it may be a challenge for you in some way.

2. Find the job description and the job advert if there is one. Bring to mind what you were told as you were invited to take on your new responsibilities, and what you have found out yourself. Reflect on what is being asked of you in this moment. As you do this, visualise (dream!) the best version of yourself either six or twelve months from now as you are succeeding in this endeavour. How are you behaving, what are you doing, what qualities do you have? Make some notes.

3. Get feedback from others to offer different perspectives. Ask how others have tripped up in this role, or in this kind of situation, in the past. Find out what differentiated previous top performers and superstars, and those that have done this well before you. Consider how circumstances and context are different now than they were before, and what may

be new about this particular situation. From the recent past ask trusted colleagues and good friends what they think your 'watch-outs' or blind spots might be. Make some notes.

4. Ask yourself what has made you successful so far. What feedback have you had from others along the way about how you have done things well? What have others appreciated about you? What qualities do you have that have made you stand out? What is it that you are doing when you are in the flow? Think of your greatest triumphs and what exactly you did that worked so well. Make some notes.

5. On a sheet of paper or on a spreadsheet write (or type) 'stop start continue' as three column headings at the top of the page. On the left write three row headings for 'knowledge, skills and attitudes'. Remember that attitudes include your beliefs and your assumptions. Review the notes that you have made and place each item you wrote down into one of the nine boxes or cells, so that you thoughtfully and honestly complete the table that you have created.

6. Think carefully about what might be missing, and what you will need to start doing that will be new for you.

7. Scan your completed table and highlight the items

that are the most critical for you to get right as you move forward. Ask yourself, what does this situation require you to learn about yourself? Talk it through with a mentor if you have one, or a coach, or a trusted and capable friend. Make some commitments to yourself and if necessary, plan some development actions based on what you have worked through.

THREE

ACCELERATE YOUR GROWTH WITH SELF-AWARENESS

"It takes courage to endure the sharp pain of self-discovery rather than choose to take the dull pain of unconsciousness that would last the rest of our lives."
Marianne Williamson

This chapter is about the development and toning of the mind-muscles we use as we build our intuitive leadership capacity. Mindful attention to what is going on inside of us will give us an edge, and speed up the acquisition of valuable experience. We will learn how to build self-awareness and understand why this is so important, and we will begin to work with structured reflection so that we take the most learning out of our experiences.

◆

David was a punchy ops exec that would explode at his team if something went wrong during a chemical manufacturing process. He came to be known as someone that would 'go pop' and everyone knew to quietly disappear into the shadows until he had calmed down. Of course, he was well intentioned and cared deeply about his work, and in many ways was very good at it. The working culture that he was responsible for creating however was unforgiving, penal and stifling. Mistakes were punished and his team lived in fear of making them.

He knew that his reactions were what he called 'salty' and could probably be managed better. Even so he justified his outbursts as the upholding of high standards.

David had no idea about why he reacted with such force to any sort of setback, and neither did he appear to have any interest in the impact he had on his colleagues. Most crucially perhaps, he had accepted that how he operated was fixed and set in stone, and that he wouldn't be able to change.

In our coaching sessions we explored all of this together. We used a research-based neuro-scientific approach to ground his understanding about how his reaction system worked (*The Chimp Paradox*, Dr Steve Peters [2]) alongside a well-accepted psychological model (Transactional Analysis, of which more in chapter 5) to add explanation for how he had come to behave in the way that he did. He began to understand that he was continuing his family patterning for when things didn't work out as expected, and he learned about how his physiology automatically took over when his standards were not met.

I remember clearly the look in his eyes as he

began to see where his outbursts came from, and his revelation that he could train himself to choose his response rather than submit to his reactions. It took focused effort on his part until by the end of the year he had reached the point where his explosions were very rare and when they did occur his genuine apology followed.

His increased level of self-awareness and new self-management skills didn't just benefit those that worked for him. His new capacity to remain calm and focused was also noticed by his colleagues at board level. His impact rose considerably as a result.

David's switch from reacting to responding is possible for all of us. These switches however can only happen with some self-awareness. It is almost impossible to change ourselves without having an awareness of how and why we behave as we do, otherwise how would we know what needs to change? In the coaching space one of the things that we do is encourage people to see things from multiple perspectives, including different ways of seeing ourselves.

Self-awareness leads to insight, and the insight provides momentum for change.

The Oxford dictionary defines self-awareness as *"conscious knowledge of one's own character and feelings",* and goes on to state somewhat ominously *"the process can be painful…"*

◆

In the first chapter we noticed how our behaviour and what we do is determined by what we are thinking and what we are feeling. Getting to know how we think and how our feelings affect us is a large part of the self that we need to become aware of. We do this by understanding our unique psychology and how our physiology works, and how they have been shaped by our biography and the culture we grew up in.

We realise how as younger people our role models gave us many of their beliefs and assumptions, and attitudes and opinions, which we largely accepted without much thought. For all of us our family or care system moulded and framed our expectations for what life and work is about.

With self-awareness we are able to see things for what they are and how they show up in the here and now, and as a result make higher-quality decisions for how to work and live. This helps us to have the impact that we want and achieve what we set out to. As we recognise when we are getting in our own way, we can make choices to move beyond our limiting patterns.

David learned what his triggers were for becoming authoritative and aggressive, and then he taught himself to recognise these triggers as they fired in real time. Then, he used self-management skills (chapter 6) to take a breath and ask one or two questions to buy himself a bit of time so that he could calm his activated nervous system. Next, he was able to shift his inner focus to his 'adult ego state' (chapter 5). In this way he changed his approach in the moment and increased his chances of reaching a good outcome.

Later on, he reflected more deeply into the authoritative pattern and understood that it was something he copied from his parents as he grew up. With this additional level of insight, he was able to make more conscious and intentional choices about how he wanted to handle pressure in the future, using a habit building process to help him (later in this chapter).

He went further still and explored just what it was that triggered his aggressive reaction. He learned that when he felt thwarted in his endeavours (he didn't get what he wanted), what to others looked like petulance to him felt like rejection, and reminded him (that part of his brain that monitors such things) how threatening this was to his younger self. With this level of insight, he was able to see his old pattern with new eyes and remind himself that it had nothing to do with the adult he is today. In a short amount of time, he was able to form and embed new habits, thus increasing his capacity to function well in high-pressure situations.

Each of these self-awareness steps will increase our effectiveness as we learn more about who we are. When we aggregate them, then over a short amount of time we can make huge strides forward.

In this way, we mature well.

As we continue maturing throughout our lives our foundations and our 'sense of self' deepens, and as a result our resilience and our capacity increases.

In our always-on and pressurised world more and more seems to be asked of us, whether this is by our board or our employer, our most significant relationships, or simply our own response to what we see around us. The work of building our foundations is important for being able to handle the challenging situations that we find ourselves in. Our responses need to be ours and ours alone, else we live permanently at the behest of others. The strength and depth of our foundations can sustain us through the changes we have to navigate. Self-awareness is an important part of our foundations.

One simple framework I often use with clients as we agree coaching goals describes three broad areas of focus. The first is the development of self-awareness. Secondly, we focus on relational awareness, the skill of getting things done with and through other people, and thirdly we look at how we can thrive in and leverage the system that we are in to achieve what we want to.

This accessible framework makes clear the inter-dependence between all three areas of focus. So, we use our self-awareness to manage effective working and personal relationships with others, so that together we can work out how to operate within the broader system and get done what we want to.

Many of the problems and failures that clients bring into coaching have their roots in some sort of psychological or emotional blind spot, rather than a lack of knowledge or insufficient smarts. When problems with others happen we tend to say "if only they had…" rather than "if only I had…" As Jung said, *'everyone carries a shadow, and the less it is embodied in the individual's conscious life, the blacker and denser it is'* [3]. Sometimes the blackness spills over and we find ourselves becoming the issue, often without noticing.

As we move into an age of ever more complexity accompanied by more and more division, the importance of how we each contribute to solutions and problems is heightened. Modern day leaders, leaders-in-waiting, and anyone wanting to influence need to know themselves well if they want more in their list of solutions than in the list of problems.

If self-awareness is so important then how much is enough? The question hints at the almost never-ending potential for analysis and the risk of tipping into self-absorption and even obsession. Realistically, we will almost certainly never get to know everything of whom we are. The answer therefore, as with so many aspects of development, lies with what is happening around us and in particular how well things are going. It is when things aren't working for which we are accountable, or that we ourselves aren't happy with, that we need to pay attention and consider how we might inadvertently be a part of the problem alongside whomever else might be involved. Or, it is when we take on something new and have to dig deeper inside ourselves to function well.

"Look out of the window when things are going well, and in the mirror when they don't."

Unknown

Self-awareness needs to be at the heart of our thinking for recognising that what got us here won't get us there.

Then we add relational-awareness to our self-awareness. We work out how to use our body language, style of communication, and choice of words, to shift things and enable everyone to move forward. When these three facets of communication are operating in sync, we can say that we are being fully congruent, and when we do this our impact is amplified and we really can make extraordinary things happen.

The Subject Object framework

Taking on the role of the observer of ourselves in whatever situation we are in as well as being immersed in the situation itself will turbo boost our aim of increasing our level of self-awareness.

The simple and powerful 'Subject Object' framework [4] emerged in science and linguistics, and in philosophy, and has successfully transferred into many aspects of one-to-one work including coaching.

In this model we are each the most important person in the centre of our world, experiencing at first hand just what it means to be who we are. In this way we are immersed as subject.

From time to time as subject we also observe ourselves, and that which we observe is the object. This is a subtle mental adjustment, and without this ability to perceive ourselves as object we will make little progress with our self-awareness. We are observing ourselves a step removed from first hand.

A good attitude as observer becomes crucial in helping to take insight and learning from seeing the object that is us. When we observe our object self, we want our attitude to be detached, curious and as far as possible neutral. We try to separate from any emotion and drama of whatever is playing out. As we experience as subject our thoughts, feelings, and behaviours, we hover over our own shoulders *watching us* think, feel, and behave.

Cultivating the ability to be both subject and object is powerful work. From a place of detachment and neutrality we are able to see our actions and behaviours differently, and to ask questions of ourselves in relation to the context that can lead to new possibilities and ideas. As you can imagine this takes practice, and the next section on reflection offers a structured way to go about the task.

We can identify the two main topics that we wish to build self-awareness of as our psychological and our emotional identity. These are the two main drivers of our behaviour and where many of the rewards for developing self-awareness will come from.

Our goal is to build psychological maturity and emotional literacy. As we do so our ability to work and live with others will get more authentic, calmer, and way more effective. The more complicated the challenge and the greater the scale of the problem, as psychologically mature and emotionally literate adults the more that we will be able to use our whole self as a tool for change.

Self-awareness is one of the key enablers for this to happen.

"The most important conversations you will ever have are the ones you will have with yourself."
David Goggins, Ultra-athlete and Author

The Art of Reflection

"Without reflection, we go blindly on our way."
Margaret J. Wheatley

We use the word reflection a lot in this book because of its crucial enabling role in learning and growth. It is worth being clear about what we mean by it and how we can do it practically and effectively.

In Chinese philosophy the three pillars of wisdom are imitation, experience, and the 'noblest' of the three, reflection. The noble art of reflection has been valued as a practice for thousands of years.

Fast-forward to the twentieth century and social scientists and psychologists such as Dewey, Schon, and Kolb have all written about the importance of reflection for learning, with the Kolb learning cycles in particular taking root in education and leadership development.

In the context of leadership and personal development we use reflection as the primary vehicle for learning from our experiences. As we seek to understand and learn from what we have done we become more effective with the myriad of decisions that we make every day. Reflection is also, as we will see in chapter 8, one of the five skills that we can develop to cultivate our own wisdom. Reflection is wisdom in action.

What then might we reflect upon, and how do we go about doing it?

It begins with an experience in which, in some way, we have been involved. We have decided that the situation merits our reflection as we suspect that it might hold some learning for us, usually as something unsuspected happened, or what we did hasn't worked, or we are left feeling dissatisfied in some way. As we will also see, we reflect to integrate and embody new skills and ideas as quickly as possible.

We have chosen reflection for our personal learning, and not, as we may be tempted, to confirm how others might have let us down. If we find ourselves with a wandering mind and reflecting on how others could have been more effective (*"if only they had"*, or *"why can't they?"*) we have gone off track. If we are looking at the broader context and the role of others aside from our role in whatever has played out, we are in the territory of review rather than reflection. Reflection is *always about our role* in whatever has played out. Your situation may enable you to help others review their role and their effectiveness in it, and they may choose (or not) to go about their own reflection, with or without your help. In the meantime, our reflection is about us, and us alone. For this reason, we use the first person, 'I' statements, when we reflect. The scope for what we might reflect on:

- Begins with what we have done and what happened as a result.
- Which stemmed from what we were thinking and what we were feeling at the time that we did it.
- These thoughts and feelings were in turn based on what we knew and didn't know, and our emotions and how we interpreted them.
- Our knowledge will have come from how we were educated, in what we have been trained to do, and in what else we have

learned.
- Our psychological personality, our level of psychological maturity, the nature of our shadow and our ego, and our emotional literacy, combined together to influence *how* and *why* we did what we did.
- Our biography and significant life events, our family of origin and the community we grew up in, helped to shape our psychology and fed us with many of our beliefs, attitudes, biases, and assumptions. For the most part we hungrily accepted them. These aspects of who we are usually sit in our unconscious and outside of our day-to-day awareness.
- Finally, most of us will have some awareness of our ancestral legacy, and the history of our nation of birth. These will have subtle shaping effects in how we see our lives, our entitlements, and our sense of justice and injustice.

All of these parts of us are potentially in play when we reflect.

Our choice therefore is what to focus on, and how deeply we wish to reflect. The answer is of course completely personal and always determined by the context. The more that is at stake, and the more that we feel that we are in the midst of something important, or even fundamental and existential, the deeper we will need to go. If it is straightforward, or day-to-day operational, it would be easy to overthink our reflection and look for patterns that simply aren't there. This judgement is ours and ours alone. Take care though, of avoiding reflecting on what we may have done for fear of seeing the harsh reality of our imperfection.

What will also influence how deeply to reflect will be our adult psychological development. Jungian psychoanalyst James Hollis writes about the importance of asking serious questions about ourselves only once our egoic identity is strong enough to be discomforted by the answers. In the meantime, there is much to be learned from working with behaviour, modern psychology, and emotion.

Some of us will be more predisposed to reflection than others. Those with an orientation for action for example, will have to work a bit harder with the quiet demands of sitting and thinking, or writing. Those with an over-defending ego may resist even the suggestion that there are improvements to make in how to operate. On the other hand, if we are even slightly psychologically wired to observe and to be curious, we may appreciate the quiet time to recharge our batteries and find it easier to slip into reflective practice. It is ultimately skill based, and something we can all learn to do regardless of our psychological preferences.

Reflection model for embedding new skills and behaviours

In chapter 9 we will examine how we can get change to stick. We will understand why change can be difficult, particularly if we are rewiring ingrained patterns and ways of operating. We can increase enormously the chances of change sticking by using a proven reflection practice.

For behavioural skill development I have used a **30-day habit-building model** successfully with my coaching clients for many years as a way to integrate and habituate new behaviours. It offers the best chance of change taking root as we speed towards the goal of 'unconscious competence'. It is a simple daily 3-step process, requiring only a small amount of time, discipline and commitment.

This practice is based around a specific behavioural goal, for example to talk less and listen more, or to not go pop when things go wrong, or to play quieter people into meetings more. Being goal specific with this model is essential, which means taking a bit of time to work out exactly what aspect of your behaviour you wish to develop.

Step 1 asks that as we begin our day, perhaps on our commute or as our first task at work, we scan the day ahead. Identify the events of the day that offer the chance to practice the new skill. Run through in your head and visualise how you want to 'be' in each event, what you are doing or not doing, saying or not saying, and what impact you want to have. Think about what might happen that could throw you off course, and have one or two ideas in your back pocket in case this happens. This is a five or so minute activity.

In **Step 2** we simply run the day, doing our best, practicing our new behaviours where we can.

Step 3 is the most important step. At the end of the working day, when we know that we will have five to ten uninterrupted minutes, we practice the skill of reflection.

The attitude that we choose as we reflect is crucial. If our attitude is not where we need it to be it is more likely that as we reflect we will simply relive the experience. This is a time for us to be kind to ourself, and detached and curious about how we operate. If we are in any way still triggered by the events of the day, take time to calm and settle the nervous system. Go for a walk outside, do some breathing exercises or some gym work, or some mindfulness. There is no place for self-criticism or self-judgement in our reflection time; these are the enemies of learning.

We will reflect using two specific questions as we look back on the events of the day.

The **first question** as we reflect on the situations

where we used new behaviours, is *"what did I do well?"* We want to claim our successes. For example, I asked three good questions (replay them in your mind), and I listened to the answers with as much presence as I have ever done (be clear about how you did this). Or, I managed to pause and calm myself before speaking when yet another manufacturing operation faltered. Or, I showed some appreciation to a colleague.

If something has not gone as we hoped it is unlikely that every single thing that we did was not great. There will be a mix of stuff that was effective and stuff that could have gone better, even if we didn't end up where we wanted to be. The first question asks that we claim the good stuff, and own what we have done well.

Secondly, we ask, *"If I had my time over again what would I do differently?"* This is the moment to acknowledge that in this particular situation we have not been as effective as we might have wanted. It is the learning question. So, begin by isolating the specific moment that things turned away from you. There might have been a silence in the dialogue that you stepped in to fill too quickly. Someone might have said something that you found ridiculous, and you reacted with a judgemental comment. A team member repeated, yet again, the same mistake and you blew up.

Whatever it was, there will have been something

that forced you out of responding and into reacting with your old patterns and way of being. If you can't see it yourself straight away, ask someone else what they saw.

Once you have isolated the moment complete the statement, *"if I had my time over again I would ..."* and then imagine yourself doing this. For example, it could be that when you were talking with a difficult colleague the point at which you said, "no, you can't do that" was when they disengaged or got argumentative. If you had your time over again you would have said, "help me to understand your thinking here".

Allow this moment of learning to sink in. Many people make notes of their daily reflections in a notebook. That's it for the day.

The next day, repeat. And the next, and the next, for thirty days. Work diligently, with kindness, and with curiosity. Capture and accumulate daily successes and daily learning.

◆

This practice is truly remarkable because not only are we reaching our development goal by repeated practice, reflection, and learning, we are also building our capacity to reflect. As we will see in chapter 9, through the process of functional neuro-plasticity we are literally rewiring the part of our brain that handles reflecting.

Then, as the weeks go by we will find ourselves reflecting unprompted. We won't have to wait until the end of the day to reflect. We will be able to reflect in real time as the event plays out *and change tack on the fly*, increasing our effectiveness dramatically. It is amazing that we can increase our brains' capacity as adult's, way beyond the age when we thought we were fully formed, mature and developed.

Furthermore, even if we are not working with a specific development goal, we can adopt a weekly or bi-weekly reflective session to check in with our broader progress. We are generally pretty good at reviewing progress against metrics and numbers, and we can complement this with a reflection on how well we are doing against the behavioural standards that we expect of ourselves.

I have used the 30-day habit builder repeatedly in my coaching practice, and can testify to its effectiveness in helping clients achieve some amazing breakthroughs. It works!

As we get more practiced in reflection we can introduce different questions to enrich our understanding of what might be going on. Coaches use these questions a lot. These can include;

- In what ways might I have contributed to this problem?
- How may it be benefitting me to continue with this ineffective way of operating?
- What is the learning that is here for me in this situation?

- Which shadow parts of me are being exercised right now?

And of course, there are many more. Leaders who are at peace with their egoic identity (chapter 5) will be comfortable having this internal dialogue, knowing that it is one of the main ways that our innate wisdom is cultivated.

Wild writing

If we get stuck in our reflection and cannot access the information that we want to, we can use a dynamic practice called wild writing to help with the unblocking. What we do in wild writing enables us to bypass our conscious thinking with all of its associated defence mechanisms and reach our deeper levels of intelligence. I have used this practice a lot for myself, and recommended it many times, always with success. We need just fifteen minutes.

It is very simple. It works like this:

- Make sure you have a few sheets of paper to write on, and a pen or pencil
- Think of a short 'lead off' sentence that will act as the prompt for your reflection. A straightforward reflective lead off sentence could be *"I misread that meeting because I…"* or *"I lost it when…"* or *"what bothered me about*

that situation is…" A deeper reflective lead off sentence might be *"This belief/assumption / pattern serves the part of me that…"* or *"If I stop [activity] I am worried that…"* or *"my fear about this situation is that…"*

- Set a countdown timer for 15 minutes
- Write your lead off sentence at the top of the page, and begin immediately by continuing the sentence
- Write quickly
- Do not:
  - Stop writing, for anything
  - Look back at what you have written
  - Worry about your handwriting
- If you go blank, write "*I have gone blank, and what I really want to say is…*" until you find your flow again
- Only stop writing once the timer alarm goes off

By writing quickly and not stopping you will overtake your rational thinking, and enable thoughts and feelings to emerge that would otherwise have stayed in your unconscious. This is a fantastic process for surfacing what would otherwise remain hidden, and is akin to speed journaling.

Reflection is one of the primary ways in which we reach our goals and of enjoy a mindful and fully conscious life where we can live to our full potential. It increases the availability of high quality information that helps us to make even better decisions for ourselves and for others.

Socrates said that an unexamined life is not worth living. Ghandi wrote *The Story of My Experiments with Truth*, the reflective autobiography of his younger life. President Obama talked often about reflection; his book *Dream of my Father* was a reflection on his public life, and he once said *"we learn from our mistakes, we do some reflection, we lick our wounds, we brush ourselves off – then we go forward, with the presumption of faith in our fellow citizens."*

SUMMARY

- Self- awareness leads to insight, and insight generates change. It helps us to see things for what they are and as a result make higher-quality decisions for how to work and live.

- Developing self-awareness will help us to reach our goal of building psychological maturity and emotional literacy, accelerating our effectiveness in whatever endeavour in which we are involved.

- We use our self-awareness to manage effective working and personal relationships with others, so that together we can work out how to operate within the broader system and get done what we want to.

- The subject object framework helps us to turbo boost our self-awareness capacity by helping us to see ourselves in a different way.

- Reflection is wisdom in action, and a crucial part of learning.

- The 30-day habit building process not only helps us to reach our development goals, it also increases our skill level of reflection.

- Wild writing is a quick and simple way to access unconscious thoughts and feelings, and to remove any blockage we might be experiencing as we reflect.

EXERCISES

1. Write down in a notebook or a journal why it is important for you to increase your level of self-awareness. Work this question until you are clear in your own mind.

2. Ask yourself which are the parts of you that you would like to become self-aware of. Once begun this can be a never-ending journey, so begin with what is of most interest to you so that the process is as enjoyable as possible. This could begin with something like *'why do I…'* or *'what is it about me that…'* or similar. Use whatever words and language feels right for you at this time.

3. Sit on a chair in a quiet room. Slow down your breathing, and as you sit there close your eyes and imagine that there is a part of your mind that is watching you from the ceiling in a corner of the room. This part of your mind is detached and objective, interested, and kind. From that point of view look at the you that is sitting in the chair, and ask your questions. For example, *'what does she, he or they think about [the situation]? Why do you act the way that you do when [x] happens? What is hard for you in this situation?'* Trust the answers that you hear in your mind. Don't over-think or second-guess

yourself. Make some notes. Repeat this practice at least a few times a week.

4. Over time, notice any recurring themes and patterns. These are what are worth paying attention to.

5. Get practiced at doing this. It cultivates the object aspect of your mind so that you can see yourself in a different way, and get another perspective on whatever is playing out. Over time you will come to know this as a key part of your intuition.

6. If you find yourself over-thinking your role in a situation, distract yourself and allow space for your deeper thoughts and feelings to emerge naturally from your unconscious. A simple way to do this is to go for a walk and to consciously spend some time gazing at your surroundings, or to play a favourite song in your head. Giving yourself something else to focus on quiets the energized part of your mind. As you set out for your walk or however you have chosen to distract yourself, set an intention for yourself to understand what the balanced perspective is for the situation, and notice what pops into your mind on your walk. Trust this inner voice as a deeper form of intelligence that might have something useful to say about the situation you find yourself in.

7. Adopt the practice of reflection as part of your life, even if this is occasional and periodic. Make a commitment to yourself to check in at least every month with how you are doing with your psychological maturity and emotional literacy.

8. Make use of the 30-day habit building exercise as you take on specific development goals.

9. To get used to wild writing, embark on a wild writing exercise right now using the lead off sentence *'I want to build my psychological maturity and emotional literacy because…'*

FOUR

WHAT RUMBLES UNDERNEATH

"Why did I do that?"

- *Anyone who has ever lived*

These next two chapters are about some of the ways in which we are each a confusing mix of psychological drives that sit underneath the polished surface that we show to the world. We will learn the language and architecture of our psychology, and build a strong sense of who we are and what makes us often tick, and sometimes tock. We will start with modern, measurable psychology, based on work done primarily in the last fifty years (although with their roots in much earlier work).

◆

Bill sat before me, knowing what he needed to do while quaking inside at the idea of doing it. He had so far managed to avoid having the difficult conversation with two of his senior leaders about their role in the organisation. When he took on the CEO role he had inherited a mess in some key areas and important changes needed to be made including to the make up of the leadership group. While the organization was fundamentally doing OK, he didn't believe he could take it forward without a higher calibre of exec.

He had worked in the organization for many years, and was bright and insightful as well as being an inspiring leader for his people. He had positive feedback about the working environment that he was slowly building, coming as it did after a toxic phase characterised by grievances and a general sense of defensiveness, underpinned by a poorly prepared strategy. To further complicate the situation, he was working with a brand new board chair and vice-chair, and other board members with close and long-standing ties with the two individuals.

There was a lot going on, with many priorities vying for his attention, and it was easy for him to keep putting off what needed to happen. Now, though, it was obvious that he was avoiding taking action.

He was more than capable of handling this type of conflict, and he knew that things would not correct themselves unless he took action. He was aware too of how not grasping the nettle looked to other people. We agreed that it would be helpful to build our understanding of the dynamics that were in play, and so I asked him if it might be possible that a part of him benefitted from not having the difficult conversations? He nodded tentatively, and so we began by taking a look at what needs he had that were being met by his inaction.

We started with and quickly found valuable insights in his psychology. We confirmed that he had a strong preference for acting with empathy, meaning that he prefers to listen first and put himself in the shoes of others. He was also fairly conflict averse and liked to reach decisions by calm discussion and agreement. Furthermore, he had quite a high psychological need for the approval of other people, stemming from growing up with strict, domineering parents that demanded that he fall into line. This blend of characteristics led to him favouring tactics that generally pleased others and didn't expose him to any kind of domineering psychological threat. He described both individuals as spiky and outspoken, exactly the kind of people that he was instinctively wary of.

The explanation for him avoiding the difficult conversations therefore lay in the way that his psychology had been shaped as a younger person. It meant that for him that to initiate a difficult high stakes conversation with tricky people and without full board backing triggered unconscious fears of rejection and disapproval. He feared conflict with his two colleagues, and risked criticism from experienced board members. It was far easier for him to just put it off for another day, and then another, and concentrate on the things that he preferred to do.

In our coaching Bill raised his level of psychological self-awareness to the point where his present-day adult self could park the old patterns and engage in some much needed clear thinking. By managing a different internal conversation he became able to make decisions and act in spite of his fear rather than be paralysed by it. He learned to go against the grain of his psychological preferences and follow through with what needed to be done.

As it turned out neither individual was surprised, and indeed appreciated the issues being bought to the surface as they had correctly read the situation anyway. One chose to retire a little earlier than planned, and the other accepted an offer that he had been sitting on. It ended as well as these things can.

Each and every day our psychologies rumble away beneath the surface, influencing everything we do from how we greet each other at the start of the day, to how we handle conflict, to how we engage with detail, to how we make our decisions, and more. Our personality is psychological, and our psychology makes the choice of whatever face we present to the world. It determines how we handle pressure and stress, and how we adapt our behaviours as a result. Away from the need to perform for others and the way that we change as we experience pressure, our true and authentic self sits quietly as our core psychological identity.

Our psychology is distinct from our behaviour. It is important to distinguish between who we are and what we do notwithstanding the causal nature of the relationship. Our psychological personality is reasonably fixed, forming as early as three years old. We can expect slow and imperceptible shifts as we age over the decades and experience what recent research is calling the 'maturity principle', with studies showing that many of us may become a bit more extraverted, emotionally stable, and conscientious.

From time to time and particularly at work we need to do things that we are not psychologically geared up to do. For example, I might prefer doing broad level visionary thinking and being creative, and yet still have to write detailed plans, work with spreadsheets, and pay attention to terms and conditions. I will have to develop competence with detail if I am to be successful, even if I don't particularly enjoy doing so.

When planning their development clients will sometimes say that they are being asked to change who they are, to alter their personality and be something that they are not. This is a misunderstanding. If we are being asked to develop a behavioural skill that conflicts with our psychological preference for how we like to work, what we are really saying is that it feels uncomfortable. Our behaviours are skills that we can build notwithstanding the nature of our personality. Anyone that has reached any sort of seniority will almost certainly have had to become adept at doing things that do not come naturally. One wouldn't want to base a career around these skills yet having to do so simply goes with the territory.

Our psychology is completely unique to us. No one else has quite the same mix and blend of personality traits just like we each do. We can like doing the same things, regard each other as close and even the best of friends, and we can give our trust to each other, and psychologically we can be as chalk and cheese.

Our uniqueness carries some risk. Because my and your psychology are invisible, it is easy for us to get frustrated with each other as we assume that what comes easily to us is easy for all. We expect that others think in the same way that we do, and that what is important for us will be important for others. In this way we fail to appreciate psychological diversity, and end up judging and criticizing others based on our psychological differences.

Since the world's first psychological lab was set up in 1879 by Wilhelm Wundt in Leipzig psychologists have made enormous strides in how we think about what makes us the people that we are. Most of us will be aware of Freud, Jung, and possibly Adler. Maybe too of Frankl and the search for meaning, Maslow and the hierarchy of needs, and Pavlov and his dogs. Millions of us will associate personality measurement with Myers Briggs (the MBTi type based questionnaire), OPQ, 16PF, The Enneagram, Lumina Spark, and countless other questionnaires.

The way that these pioneers have studied and 'measured the mind' - identified personality traits and types and ways to assess them, and then related them to how we live and perform at work - has brought us to a place whereby psychological thinking has deep and broad practical application. Psychological personality assessments are a key part of the array of tools used to determine how well suited an individual might be for a job. Anyone at a senior level will most likely have completed several in the course of their careers.

Being aware of how our psychology and our psychological preferences shape what we do and why we do it enables us to make clean decisions, uninfluenced by our quirks and idiosyncrasies.

Imagine having to make a rapid decision with incomplete information in a high stakes situation. We might tremor nervously at the thought or bubble with excitement. It could be a medical emergency, dealing with a defective and unsafe product, handling a catastrophic oil spill, or facing a challenging question in front of our peers from someone opposing us about a contentious topic. Our personal reputation might be on the line.

Imagine too that our psychological personality is relatively competitive, that we have a strong preference for making decisions based on solid evidence, and that we have low levels of empathy. Perhaps also we are willing to engage in conflict as we imagine that this makes us appear 'strong' and in command. These traits are typical in ambitious and successful people.

With this kind of psychological profile, we will struggle to make a quick decision with missing information. If we need to concede on something or admit a failure our need to win can strangle any idea of movement. As we need to bring people with us our lack of empathy and enjoyment of the argument may repel the very people that we need to stay on board. And there are many more psychological dynamics that could trip us up.

These psychological needs are often unconscious even as they colour and influence how we operate. Being aware of our preferences allows us to choose the best way of behaving so that we can reach the outcomes that we want to. With experience and self-awareness we can learn to operate *against* our psychology, if we deduce that this will be necessary to get things done.

The strides made in the last century about human psychology are extraordinary. Psychological personality assessments offer rich data upon which we can build our understanding of our personality and how we like to operate. The information they reveal adds considerable value in helping us figure out how we can become stronger performers, more credible candidates, better leaders, more effective co-workers, and for building our careers in the way that we wish to.

Sitting underneath the personality that we show and the behaviours that we use are deeper psychological levers and pulleys that are important in our maturing and growth. Let's take look now and in the following chapter at some of the thinking that over the years has resonated most strongly with clients in my coaching practice.

"I suppose it is tempting, if the only tool you have is a hammer, to treat everything as if it were a nail."
- *Abraham Maslow, Psychologist*

Adult (vertical) development

Over the last fifty years we have made huge progress in understanding how we continue to develop as adults, heavily influenced by the first wave of psychologists and psychoanalysts. It used to be accepted that once we reached adulthood, then from a psychological perspective that was it, we were fully formed and considered mature. How wrong we were!

We now know how we grow and change psychologically, aside from our stable psychological personality. Growth throughout adulthood can be charted in stages, potentially right up until the moments of old-age and death. It is in the discipline of adult, or vertical, development that we can look to for insights about this type of growth, as we think about what kind of leadership we need for these complex and troubling times, as well as what kind of leader and person we have the potential to grow in to.

As we develop throughout adulthood our attitude toward and balance between what we could think of as "I" and "us" changes. At the broadest level the idea of a first and a second half of psychological life (which later came to be known as the conventional and post-conventional stages of life by the likes of Kohlberg [5], and then Wilbur, Kegan, Loevinger and others) was first suggested by Carl Jung. One of his many insights was that we spend the first half of our psychological adulthood establishing ourselves professionally and personally, such that we tend to be more self-focused, ambitious, perhaps selfish and even ruthless, and acquisitive (of status and stuff). During this phase we are developing and strengthening our ego, our sense of our individual self.

Something then might happen that forces us take stock. It could be a job failure, a divorce, or an illness. It may be that we look at our status and our stuff and are shocked to realise that our success hasn't satisfied us in the way that we expected. We then find ourselves asking some serious questions about who we are and what the point of all of our hard work is. We no longer feel so clear about our core beliefs and assumptions. There is some debate about whether we have to experience something challenging and difficult to catalyse this type of growth, or whether we can develop intentionally without this. The evidence for the latter is light, and I tend to go with the necessity of a challenging experience simply because most of us are either too busy, too comfortable, or too identified with our success to want to rip up a part of the old self and start anew. Most of us need to be made to pay attention.

If and when that challenging event does happen it can feel as if we are at a major crossroad, and being asked to make some important choices. For some of us our first choice may be to avoid the question, and so we double down and try to make the old self work better. Some of us however will take a deep breath and bravely accept what feels like an invitation addressed to the deeper parts of who we are. We somehow know that we cannot continue as before and that we simply have to step forward into a different way of being, and living, and working. In these moments we take our first hesitant steps into the second half of our psychological life, where it is less about 'me' and more about 'us'.

There are many frameworks and models to help us to understand where we are with our adult development, and what a different way of being might look like. For leaders in organizations Harthill [6] have developed the Leadership Development Framework (LDF), based on the works of Rooke and Torbert that defines growth through seven stages. It reminds us that even as we develop we still lean into old patterns and stages depending on what is going on. In this work what matures is how we interpret our surroundings and how we react when our power or safety is challenged.

Susan Cook-Greuter [7] is one of the modern pioneers of adult development and ego maturation, and designed the Leadership Maturity Framework along with Beena Sharma. They highlight how as we develop as adults we see the world through new eyes and change our interpretations of our experiences to transform our view of reality.

This framework also highlights how our attitude to feedback can be a barometer for our level of adult maturity. Feedback can feel like a serious challenge to our power and safety, as highlighted by Rooke and Torbert. From total resistance and rejection of feedback at our youngest and earliest stages, through grudging acceptance and then more willing acceptance as we mature, to engagement and interest, into genuine curiosity and searching for feedback, and finally to a state of paying attention to everything as potential sources of feedback. It is insightful work.

In her early work Cook-Greuter described the step from the first to the second half of life as akin to moving from an ego state of knowledge to an ego state of wisdom. As research and thinking has delivered new interpretations the number of adult development stages has shifted from seven to eight, and even to nine stages. Regardless of the model or how many stages there are, the importance of the transition from the first to the second half of life is consistent.

Not all of us will grow through all of the stages. In fact, fewer of us will move into the second half of psychological life than remain in the first. A 2002 (restated in 2014 [8]) study by Cook-Greuter finds that a mere 15% of the US population are in the post-conventional (second half) stages of psychological adult maturity. Furthermore, the two halves of life are not even split chronologically, as if we will reach forty and then flip over. As we look across all walks of life we will sometimes see leaders with serious responsibility, and yet without the adult maturity that the job requires and only a fledgling relationnship with their own power and safety.

The pivot from the first to the second half of life then, is the moment when we start to question our hitherto relentless focus on the self to the exclusion of others, and begin the relocation of the self within society and community. For some of us, particularly if we are psychologically wired to be competitive, driven, and achievement oriented, this is a lifelong process of balancing our psychological needs. Even as we develop we still have our basic psychological personality drives and motivations.

Barrett Brown described post-conventional leaders as *"able to take a systems view and even a unitive view of reality: simultaneously hold and manage conflicting frames, perspectives and emotions; and deeply accept oneself, others, and the moment, without judgement. Such individuals also report deep access to intuition and perceive their rational mind as a tool, not as a principal way to understand reality. They appear to heavily tolerate uncertainty and even collaboratively engage with ambiguity to create. Finally, they experience frequent 'flow' and 'witnessing' states of consciousness."* [9]

I have quoted this verbatim for its profound importance as we consider what kind of leadership we need for the current age. In Browns research he found that sustainability initiatives led by psychologically mature leaders had the design of the initiatives deeply grounded in transpersonal meaning, or meaning located externally rather than internally. In addition, they used intuition alongside rational ways of knowing, and engaged with the collective and the system as well as those directly involved.

This shift between the two broad stages of life is also reflected in Spiral Dynamics, a society level map of the evolution of human consciousness begun by Clare Graves in the 1960's and taken on by Beck and Cowan who then designed the framework. It articulates eight different world-views that we each have the potential to hold. The underlying motive in the first six (tier 1) world-views can be regarded as being based in fear, and the motive in the last two (tier 2) as based in love. In the first tier people find it difficult to understand those who have differing world-views and generally oppose and fight to win, while in the second tier there is an understanding and appreciation for all world-views as they each have their relevance and place, and generally unite and look for win-win outcomes.

The shift to post-conventional can be confusing and humbling as we acknowledge that what we used to be certain about is now up for grabs. It can be a time of mid-life crisis, or indeed any-time crisis. Some of us may be lucky enough to sail through relatively unscathed, and some of us might hit the rocks.

To a leader in the second half of life the holding of power becomes an awesome responsibility rather than the rightful reward for hard work and the defeat of rivals. The authority of a position allows collective ambitions to be realised rather than personal dreams to be celebrated and defended at all costs.

In authentic leadership thinking, an authentic leader's conviction and drive is matched by their humility and collective attitude towards others (Neil Crofts 2006 [10]). Conviction and drive without humility can easily slip into arrogance. Humility without conviction and drive can appear weak. The blend of both however is compelling.

The transition from the first to the second half of life has also been called the moment at which we 'surrender to love'. There is no stronger drive for us humans than the feeling of love. What place does this language have in modern leadership thinking? In our context this is love in its broadest sense with its roots in mystical thinking, as an acknowledgement of the inherent mystery of what life is all about. By surrendering to love we are accepting our smallness in the broader scheme of things while retaining our connection with just what it is to be human.

We understand that we are each simultaneously completely ordinary and uniquely extraordinary, and are accepting and surrendering to the idea that there are many things over which we have no control and only a limited understanding. Despite this we carry on as best we can regardless, somehow trusting that all will be well. It is not romantic love, and it does not preclude being tough minded, assertive, and clear with others. It is an *attitude* laced through with humility, kindness, and compassion. Furthermore, it sits side by side with our psychological personality and the rough (or too smooth) edges that the vast majority of us have acquired in growing up. When we own, integrate and embody all of these parts of ourselves, we are real and convincing. We are neither with our head in the clouds, or stuck in the drama of whatever is playing out. To be real, as you can imagine, takes a lot of work. We begin the surrender to love as we enter the second half of life.

Adult development is one of the most important

ways to think about maturity of attitudes and has a major influence on our outlook, how we see ourselves, how we make decisions and how incredibly effective we have the potential to become.

We need as many leaders as possible in the second half of their life.

"Maturity is the ability to postpone gratification."
- *Sigmund Freud*

SUMMARY

- Our psychological personality and identity are separate from our behaviour. Being aware of how our psychology and our psychological preferences shape what we do and why we do it enables us to make clean decisions.

- With experience and self-awareness we can learn to operate both with, and *against* our psychology as necessary.

- Growth throughout adulthood can be charted in stages, potentially right up until the moments of old-age and death. As we develop as adults we see the world through new eyes and change our interpretations of our experiences to transform our view of reality.

- To a leader in the second half of life the holding of power becomes an awesome responsibility rather than the rightful reward for hard work and the defeat of rivals. The authority of a position allows collective ambitions to be realised rather than personal dreams to be celebrated and defended at all costs.

- We need as many leaders as possible in the second half of their life.

EXERCISES

1. If you work for an organisation ask to complete a psychological personality questionnaire for your professional development, and request a debrief from a qualified practitioner. This will offer insights about your own psychological preferences at work and boost your self-awareness, such that you can make better quality decisions. It will also help you to understand how we are each different, making us more accepting of the ways that we each operate.

2. If you don't have this option, you can access many of the better-known questionnaires online (see note [11]). Some of them are available free of charge. Look online also for a qualified practitioner to debrief the report so that you get a good understanding of it. Many firms have links by geography to trained practitioners.

3. As above, this time for an adult (vertical) development assessment [12]. The market for adult development assessments is far smaller. These assessments take longer to complete and interpret, and consequently cost more, however the insights are incredibly rich and valuable. As with personality questionnaires it is very important to debrief the report with a qualified and experienced practitioner

so that you get a proper interpretation and thorough understanding of your profile, and how it fits in with earlier and later steps of adult psychological maturity. This assessment will highlight your current vertical psychological profile, and signpost further steps that are open to you with focused effort and practice.

FIVE

THE RATS FIGHTING IN A SACK

"If you get the inside right, the outside will fall into place."
- Eckhart Tolle

Next, we will take a look through three different lenses to shape our understanding of the deeper psychological aspects of who we are. The latest of these is from sixty plus years ago, before we step into the shadow and the ego; a very different landscape from the psychology of the last chapter.

◆

Transactional Analysis (TA)

Malene was a successful Danish country lead for a pharma company with an opportunity to take on a bigger role in Germany. She applied for the job and prepared well, was assessed and interviewed, and sadly failed to get the appointment. She was crushed. Not just disappointed and then slowly able to dust herself down kind of crushed, but almost existentially devastated. Her reaction was way of out of proportion to what had happened. We set about looking for possible explanations so that she could understand what might be going on, and as a result bounce back.

We began a discussion about success and rejection and how this had showed up for her as a younger person. It turned out that Malene had been raised by her father to be the best at pretty much everything that she did whether this was academics, sports, and even leisure. The only way to gain her father's approval was to succeed. The alternative for her as a child was cold rejection and the withholding of paternal love, which to her as a child was unthinkable and so she pushed herself harder and harder to never experience it.

As we fast-forward into adulthood Malene's pattern continued in her career, pushing herself to do well and always reaching the goals she had set for herself. Until the German opportunity. It was the first time she had not reached her goal. Somehow the dynamics that she grew up with burst into the open leaving her feeling just as she had as a young person fighting hard to win her father's approval. The interview panel that had appointed someone else and who in the process had rejected her were hundreds of miles away and it was unlikely she would interact with them again. She was left with her overwhelming feelings of rejection and didn't know what to do with them.

This was one of those coaching situations that

tipped over into therapy, and Malene found a local counselor to work with that helped her to neutralise the effects of the past and rebalance herself.

In important ways the experience taught her something about herself that being successful could never have done, and set her up for the next phase of her life and career with a greater level of wisdom and self-awareness. As a result she became even more convincing, and is now happily settled and thriving in her next role.

It is helpful to understand why we behave as we do, particularly when we know that we aren't handling events around us as well as we would like to. TA [13] is a psychological framework from the late 1950's created by Canadian psychologist Eric Berne that helps to build an understanding about how our formative years have shaped the way that we react to present day situations. At a headline level it is easy to grasp and makes perfect sense, and I have hardly ever known a client that didn't immediately begin recalling memories of how their past influences their present. It is a great way to build our awareness about one of the ways that our psychology was shaped in the first place.

One of the key aspects of the framework (there are several) would say that at any time we are all in one of three ego states. These are the 'parent, the adult, and the child ego states', acronymed as PAC.

That is to say that present moment events can trigger deep and old memories of situations that had similar characteristics and dynamics. In the here and now these memories unconsciously elicit the responses that we used back then to stay feeling safe, via our brains limbic system and specifically something called the amygdala. The amygdala is a legacy from the time when we hunted and were nomadic, and is at the heart of our 'fight flight freeze' reaction mechanism. It has just one purpose, which is to keep us alive.

As an example, if I had a domineering or even bullying parent or caregiver, as a younger person I might have reigned in my naturally ebullient behaviour to please whoever was dominating me. I would have done this to get their approval and therefore their care since I was totally dependent on them. Now, years later as an adult, if I encounter a domineering and overly directive colleague - it doesn't even have to be a boss - I might unconsciously adopt the same kind of pleasing way of operating and slip into my child ego state. I might have some idea that I am not standing up for myself, yet I won't have a clue as to why.

Malene had been thrown into the turmoil of her child ego state by her first significant adult experience of rejection.

What is going on is that the part of our brain that scans for threat – the amygdala – does its scanning job and in milliseconds recalls old memories. It matches what it sees in the present with what it remembers from the past, assumes it is a real threat, and triggers the same physiological reaction that it used to *whether or not this is necessary or appropriate*. Unfortunately for us the amygdala isn't bothered about how this affects our performance at work or what it makes us look like. It is our internal first level reaction unit and leaves the rational and relational stuff to other parts of our brain. It fires first and instantaneously, way more quickly than the parts of our brain that manage reason and smart thinking, and for this reason it can feel like we are out of control.

Another example might be of being in a situation where we have to get something done by working with or through other people. If it isn't going well and we need to hold some folks to account the same process might kick in. This time however, our amygdala might recall how we watched other people handle similar situations when we were far younger, for example how we were treated when we misbehaved or we didn't do our tasks and chores. If they became authoritative, judgemental, and maybe even aggressive with us, we might unconsciously adopt these behaviours ourselves and in doing so slip into the parent ego state. The expression *'I open my mouth and my mother/father comes out'* describes this well.

An important dynamic plays out within these three ego states. When I am in my parent ego state, I am unconsciously inviting those around me to adopt their child ego state and submit to me. In the parent ego state my psychological aim is to dominate. Conversely when I am in the child ego state I am unconsciously inviting others to get into their parent ego state and dominate me. My psychological aim in the child ego state is to gain approval and feel safe. When we are in our child ego state we are more likely to behave either passively or rebelliously, and when we are in our parent ego state others are likely to experience us as either aggressive or nurturing.

We are at our best when we are in our adult ego state. If we want others to operate from their adult ego state – to be clear, assertive, and respectful – we need to be in our own adult ego state, otherwise it becomes virtually impossible.

It is important to understand that when we are in the child or parent ego state, we are not being childish or parental; instead, we are unconsciously using reactions from the past to stay feeling safe and in control in the present.

These dynamics happen all of the time. In most days we will spend time in each of the three ego states. Usually, these moments when we are not in the adult ego state pass us by without any drama. Sometimes however, it gets in the way. Say that a key decision needs to be made and there are strong and opposing views about how to handle something. If we have been 'at it' for a while we may be tired, or we could have issues outside of work preying on our minds. Depending on the memories our amygdala retrieves, coupled with the way that our unique psychology adapts to stress and pressure, we may either appease and cave in too easily or try to steamroll our way through by force of will. Our adult ego state can be elusive as we battle with our internal reactions to the combination of complex challenge and pressure.

Our goal as decision makers and leaders is to remain in the adult ego state as much as possible – to be the 'adult in the room' - and to recognise when we have shifted into either the parent or child ego state by using our self-awareness and reflection skills. When the heat is on this can be hard to do. Chapter 6 offers some proven tactics to help us manage our internal reactions.

<u>Shadow</u>

Modern psychology gives us much to work with. Scientific research has led to assessment methods with reliability and validity, or what us non-scientists might think of as the repeatability and effectiveness of whatever approach we might be using. It is easy to slip into the mindset that if something isn't measured it can't be of any use, however there is richness in some aspects of psychology that are harder to pin down.

Here, we are in the territory of the shadow and the ego. We will have heard of these things. Freud and Jung have written about them. Their ideas and concepts have high *face* validity, meaning that for many of us they simply make good sense and feel right. We have not as yet though been able to measure them. As this is being written there are dozens of live research projects across the world into the existence and nature of consciousness, wrestling for example with the question of whether consciousness is a product of the brain, or the other way around. Perhaps one day we will get some answers, and in the meantime we can still be sure that we have something called consciousness. The absence of evidence does not always deny a reality.

In that vein we can be sure that our shadow and our ego exist. Sometimes they shout loudly and affect our decision-making, and perhaps they shout the loudest of all in those who have fought the hardest and made the biggest sacrifices to achieve their lofty career ambitions.

Beginning then with the shadow, we can start by asking what exactly it is. Most of us have probably heard of it as something nefarious and suspect that it might be up to no good. Robert Bly in his *A Little Book on the Human Shadow* [14] describes it as *"the dark side of a personality"*, and *"the long bag we drag behind us heavy with the parts of ourselves our parents or community didn't approve of"*. Grisly stuff indeed; we all have our shadow lurking in the background.

Exposing our shadow to light is another way of increasing our level of self-awareness. It can help to propel us forward as we learn to neutralize some of the ways in which we get in our own way. Our shadow is found in our blind spots, sitting there beneath our conscious awareness. It is the deeper parts of ourselves that we wished we didn't have, most likely due to times when in the past we might have been shamed, criticized, judged, or punished.

Our shadows show up in many ways. For example, when we don't get our own way and feel thwarted, and we either crumble or throw a fit. When we are faced with threat and we fight back with a disproportionate level of fury. Or when we have to speak up and our voice creeps out apologetically. Maybe there are situations when we are expected to express some kind of emotion and we go blank, or when we need to stand up for ourselves and we can barely leave our chair. There are many more ways and they all reveal how we have suppressed important parts of how we express ourselves, and then here we are as adults remaining muted or acting inappropriately.

The shadow rears up and shows its face without our being aware. It is a paradox. To look for the shadow or a blind spot is to search for…what?

There is a story in Robert MacFarlane's book *Underland* [15] about a scientist working deep beneath sea level off the Yorkshire coast in the UK, tucked away in a quiet corner within a vast underground salt and potash mining system. The scientist is looking for evidence of almost impossibly small dark matter (wryly referred to as WIMPS, or a weakly interacting massive particles) by searching for the tiny collisions that these WIMPS have with baryonic matter, or the very slightly bigger stuff that we can detect and measure. It is a great metaphor for working with the shadow. Rather than looking for the shadow itself we can notice the ripples, impacts and collisions in our life situations, and that richest of compost, our failures. We can piece together the identity of our shadow by looking at our clumsiness, our avoidances, our dissatisfactions, our reactions, and our deepest fears.

For example, why do I find it hard to show genuine appreciation to tired colleagues that have done a great job, instead exhorting them to deliver even more? How come I can't abide looking stupid or clownish and will avoid any situation where this might happen? Why do I push myself to do such a perfect job until late in the evening, every day of the week? Why do I need to control other people so much? We each have our own patterns and blind spots.

The answers to these and similar questions will take us back to what was denied us when we were younger. In Robert Bly's language these will be the identity parts of our psyche that we chopped off and put in the sack, that from that moment on we carry around with us over our shoulder. In the second half of our psychological life we will spend time attempting to empty the sack. Perhaps I was judged and criticised for showing appreciation, or I was laughed at and shamed for extravagantly expressing myself. Maybe if I was at last praised for something I determined to be the best ever at that thing and my perfectionism was born. Or if others repeatedly diminished me I could grab some kind of feeling of safety by then telling whomever I could what to do. We didn't consciously choose these tactics, we simply came to rely on them as coping mechanisms, and then decades later here they still are, popping up when we least expect them to.

Making time for contemplation and reflection can flush out the information that begins to put shape and form to our shadow. In particular, taking a step back and looking for our repeating patterns offers clues to our shadow identity and how it shows its face. Doing this with a qualified and experienced counselor or therapist is likely to be even more productive.

Some years ago I did my own shadow work with Marianne Hill [16], a highly experienced practitioner. The legacy of my maternal relationships as a child had affected how I engaged with independent, capable and yet emotionally distant women, and through just one session of shadow work this aspect of how I operate was transformed. It felt genuinely miraculous and liberating. At last I was able to define and manage healthy boundaries with positive impacts for my working and personal relationships with these kind of people. I no longer allowed my shadow based unconscious reactions to get in the way of whatever needed to get done.

Ego

Sitting alongside our shadow we need to become familiar too with our ego. The word is thrown around a lot, usually as an insult. We never seem to compliment someone on his or her ego, even though it has a crucial role for us.

Many of the systems in organisations and in society reward egocentric behaviour. These systems attract those that seek power for its status, rewards, or simply for its ability to have power over others, and then communities, and eventually even countries. Status is a currency of power in hierarchies.

Douglas Adams (author) observed *"it is a well-known fact that those people who must want to rule people are, ipso facto, those least suited to do it...anyone who is capable of getting themselves made President should on no account be allowed to do the job"*.

The word ego ("I myself" in Latin) is attributed to Freud, and is a part of his description of how our psyche is organised, alongside the id and the super-ego. Its ongoing job is as mediator between these two other two concepts. The ego does this by carrying out important roles for us, for example in performing executive functions such as reasoning and applying common sense, and most importantly for us, in concerning itself with our psychological safety. All of this is vital and necessary for our normal and healthy functioning.

However, as the ego takes on responsibility for our psychological safety we can 'over-defend' against what our developing ego and emerging sense of self regards as a threat. This over-defending gets in the way of us building a legitimately healthy ego and mature sense of our identity. We can recall that one of our first half of life aims is to establish ourselves amongst our personal and professional peers, and we acquire whatever importance we can as a part of this process. Over defending mechanisms include denial, fantasy, repression, and many more. Popular thinking about the ego has come to see it as identified with self-esteem and an inflated sense of self-worth, and even with entitlement, and this is what we see when an ego is over-defending. Iris Murdoch referred wonderfully to the over-defending ego as *"the anxious avaricious tentacles of the self"*.

What does this mean for our psychological self-awareness, leadership, and our maturing? We can see that individuals with high levels of drive and intelligence, with a sense of entitlement acquired over many years of strengthening and over-defending, reinforced in educational and family systems, can struggle to collaborate, show vulnerability, take direction, listen, engage with difference, and many of the other crucial relational skills necessary in a modern, complex, interdependent world.

Iris Murdoch's quote resonates so strongly because it reveals the fragility of the over-defending ego. The sadness buried at the heart of this is that the defence mechanisms that we use are intended to ward off troubling feelings of anxiety. We can end up with an outer brittleness that disguises an inner emptiness, as the individual struggles with their real sense of who they are, their "I myself". This inner emptiness has shallow roots and is no way to build a resilient, sustaining and enriched life. Moreover, the rest of us can see through this kind of facade even if we are afraid of or threatened by it. We humans, it turns out, have sophisticated radars and threat detection mechanisms, and it has profound implications for if and how we follow those who are supposed to be leading us.

Again, the work of reflection and contemplation, the use of failure as a vehicle from which to learn and grow, become the means by which we can begin to make sense of our confusing interior. The inflated ego is a sure sign of someone navigating the first half of his or her psychological life, as they establish and reinforce their sense of themselves and their identity. The stronger and more impregnable the ego the greater the deflation if they ever begin to explore post-conventional living and working, or contemplate the surrender to love necessary for 'tier two' deeper adult maturity. The work of knowing what we stand for, and why, can unlock valuable insights from our biography. We will look at this in greater depth in chapter 7.

Working with TA, and the shadow and ego is the work of mining for psychological gold. On the other side awaits wisdom, humility, and that rare leadership ability, to achieve far more by doing less, with more presence and using less force. As we slowly lose our attitudes of superiority and inflated feelings of being special, our arrogance is replaced by a more convincing kind of strength, and that is the moment that we begin to learn how to use the self as a tool for change.

"Ego interrupts intuition."

- *Danielle Laporte.*

SUMMARY

- Transactional Analysis is a psychological framework that helps build an understanding about how our formative years have shaped the way that we react to present day situations. We are at our best when we are in our adult ego state.

- Our shadow is found in our blind spots, sitting there beneath our conscious awareness. It is the deeper parts of ourselves that we wished we didn't have, most likely due to times when in the past we might have been shamed, criticized, judged, or punished.

- Exposing our shadow aspects to light can propel us forward as we gain deeper levels of self-awareness, and learn to neutralize some of the ways in which we get in our own way.

- A healthy ego is essential for functioning well. It is when our ego over-defends that we mis-use power and shackle our strengths.

- We 'over-defend' against what our developing ego regards as a psychological threat, as a way to ward off troubling feelings of anxiety.

EXERCISES

1. Using the daily practice of reflection (chapter 3), for as little as five to ten minutes look back on the day and identify the moments when you weren't at your best relationally or interpersonally (it is usually when we are with others that our patterns show up). Excuse yourself if you were simply tired or distracted by important events in your life. Acknowledge that most of us are trying to do our best most of the time. As you reflect ask yourself what it was that knocked you off track, or what triggered you and affected how you were with other people. Make short notes.

2. After a few weeks, look for any patterns or themes that are emerging and make connections to TA, shadow, and/or ego. Use whichever of these themes that resonates most strongly for you. This is a gentle enquiry designed to surface patterns that you might have, and that you can explore more deeply if you choose to.

3. If the pattern(s) merit deeper enquiry, it pays dividends to talk them through with someone else. You could start with a trusted friend or partner and get some feedback about what they see. Ultimately it can be enormously helpful to talk it through with

an experienced and trained professional, either in the coaching or the counseling space. The goal is simply to increase your level of your self-awareness about your psychological identity and history so that you can make decisions that increase your level of effectiveness and impact.

4. Consider specific depth shadow work with a trained and experienced practitioner.

SIX

HAVE YOU GOT THE COURAGE TO BE HUMAN?

"There is no separation of mind and emotions; emotions, thinking and learning are all linked."
- *Dr Eric Jensen, Social Scientist*

This chapter is about our emotions and feelings and why it is super-important for us to engage with them. We will come to understand that as we do so we will live far more enriched and fully functioning lives. We will be able to trust our intuition more, increasing our leadership capacity. It offers explanation for our emotions and how critical they are for our normal day-to-day work and our decision making, and encourages us to pay attention to strong emotions in ourselves and in others. We will consider our emotions as a means by which we can access our natural, physiological intelligence.

◆

Geoff sat in front of me, shifting uncomfortably in his chair as he relayed the feedback his team had shared with him after his first few months as exec director of sales and marketing. They had talked with him about his personal behaviour and porous boundaries, and were feeling angry and confused. We set about thinking how to move forward.

He had a mandate to shake things up and was happy to ruffle a few feathers along the way. With that in mind he was clear that he wanted to get his leadership team working well, and prioritized a team session over individual work. We agreed that I would speak with each of his team to get a sense of the problems from their perspective along with their expectations, and then work closely with Geoff to build the content for a team working day. As the issues only exploded into life much later this seemed OK as a way forward.

Along with the usual gripes about clunky processes and frustration about some people, the team member prep calls hinted at broken promises and Geoff's poor behaviour while stopping short of giving anything concrete to work with. Despite some probing and assurances of anonymity I was unable to tease out any specifics. What was becoming clear was that the trust that had taken years to establish under his predecessor had all but evaporated in a few short months, and the atmosphere in the leadership group was charged and uncomfortable. While we had enough to build the team session I confided with Geoff that there were some underlying issues that remained unclear. Without more information we were taking a big risk with his objectives for the day. Could we postpone the group work and instead run an individual development programme beginning with him as leader, supported by some 360-feedback data? He swerved the question and put the feedback down to the loyalty they felt to his predecessor, and their reluctance to adapt to new ways of doing business.

The team day was set up to enable a transition from the old culture and way of working to something new and included a re-contracting with each other, all based around the challenging targets they were working with. Interdependence within this team was critical, more than most actually, and as a result of the leadership change they had each retreated into their own caves and silos. They needed to re-engage with each other and work out the gives and gets, as well as their joint mission and collective identity under new leadership.

The day arrived and the sessions began. The pressure that had been building held for less than an hour before it erupted and burst into the open. In the safety of the group people began to say what they had been unwilling to share in our prep calls, and an angry finger-pointing discussion ensued with accusations being freely hurled around, all aimed at Geoff. To his enormous credit he didn't bite back, and once it had calmed down a bit, we took a break so that we could figure out how to adapt the agenda and work with the heat that was in the room.

We began again. The emotion gave way to clear

examples of Geoff's personal behaviour and the impact that it was having across the function and beyond. How he dealt with them would set the tone for how they could move forward, and he began to engage at the emotional level as well as with the actual behaviours. His team sat back and listened with a kind of hopeful skepticism. The atmosphere in the room felt as if it was finely balanced as on a knife edge, and in the end, sadly, they were right to be skeptical.

As Geoff responded it become clear that he was consumed with *his* guilt, shame, and remorse for how he had breached their trust and let them down. He didn't acknowledge the distress being felt by his team, some of who had covered for and mopped up after him. Being wrapped up in his own emotions he came across as self-absorbed, lacking in empathy and ultimately weak. In those moments he lost the team. I tried to steer it back to what it meant for them but they saw straight through this and the one opportunity he had to begin the hard work of rebuilding trust had gone begging. Anger gave way to contempt, when it could have led to the start of some much needed healing.

The team never recovered, and he lasted only a few more months before moving on.

Sitting alongside psychological self-awareness is our ability to engage with our and others' emotions, and it is our emotional literacy that gives them a voice. Daniel Goleman writes, *"for better or worse, intelligence can come to nothing when the emotions hold sway"* [17]. Most of us have been overwhelmed by our or others' emotions at some point in our lives, and we know how destabilizing and all-consuming they can be. Being able to work with emotions rather than ignoring or suppressing them can enable us to remain super-effective when the heat is on, and as a result be able to make better decisions.

We are sometimes told that emotions are the enemy of reasoned thinking and have no part in decision-making. Reductive thinking has emotion and rational thinking in opposition, pitted against each other. We rightly expect decisions to be well thought through taking into account a range of different perspectives, to be 'gamed out' using various assumptions, and with some awareness of what the unknowns might be. We want risks to be assessed, and soft as well as hard factors to be considered. All of this is sensible, necessary, often brilliant work, and is the stuff of business schools and much of leadership development.

Many of us also want decision-makers to make a genuine connection with whoever might be following their leadership. Skilled leaders are plugged in to their own and others emotions, elevating their impact beyond dry, intellectual or even dominant ways of persuading and influencing.

The important role of emotions in decision-making has been proven in many studies. Antoine Bechara at the University of Iowa published a study in 2004 [18] that found that people with injuries to certain parts of their pre-frontal cortex result in impairments to their decision-making process, *"the process of decision-making depends in many important ways on neural substrates that regulate homeostasis, emotion, and feeling"*. In other words, the parts of the brain responsible for our emotions and feelings are crucial in the way that we make decisions. In all walks of life we ignore emotion at our peril.

Emotional intelligence, or EQ, is the ability to perceive, express, and manage emotions, in the self and in others. There are various EQ models, usually comprising these four components:

- o Self-awareness, self-perception
- o Self-management, expression and containment of emotions
- o Stress management, harnessing feelings
- o Relationship management, regard for others

Unlike our psychology our EQ slowly and noticeably increases as we gather experience and age, peaking sometime in our later mid life. Disentangling our EQ from our psychology however is tricky as any correlation between EQ and performance is all but impossible to separate from the impact of our psychology, at least at the moment. In this way EQ and psychology are as siblings in the psyche, closely related while remaining quite different. Psychological self-awareness and emotional literacy combine with our intellect to give rise to the most potent and skilled form of leadership. Daniel Golemans groundbreaking work *"Emotional Intelligence and why it matters more than IQ"* (note 15) remains a vital and important source of rich material. It is plugged in to many frameworks and assessment methods and is widely accepted by many mainstream organizations as desirable to essential depending on the culture and attitude of the leadership.

Leaders that 'get' us and take who we are into account generate more trust than those that don't, whether we are alone with them in the room or as part of a crowd in a group session. In this way a leaders EQ is positively linked with psychological safety and trust building, which in turn generates engagement and commitment.

Emotions, feelings, and physiology

The words feeling and emotion are often used interchangeably and yet contain an important difference. We can think of emotions as sensations that arise in our body based on physiological reactions, for example a flood of adrenalin or the rush of endorphins, or the drip of oxytocin or cortisol. Our body rapidly changes as a result; our cheeks can flush red and our hearts start pumping blood more quickly, we might sweat, our minds can go blank, our breathing shallows, and we gain tension in our muscles. These changes are our body's way of preparing us for action. In evolutionary terms we experience emotions to make us do something, whether this is fighting off a predator, running fast to catch prey, or to find a mate.

Feelings take the emotion and apply a mental filter to aid our comprehension of what is going on. For example, we meet someone new at a party and notice that we are becoming flushed, or our breathing is becoming constricted, or our stomach is tensing. Some of us will feel excited at the prospect of a new friend, or more, while others might feel awkward or even intimidated. The physiological response will be the same – flushed cheeks, constricted breathing, tense stomach – yet the mind applies a different interpretation based on our psychology, the context, and our past experience.

Emotions are the raw data. Feelings are our interpretation of the data. In this way our emotions perform a vital role and are critical for our survival, and to our ability to function well in relation to others and what is going on around us. We would find it impossible to get through the day, making the myriad of decisions that we do, without our emotions. They bring a different form of intelligence to how we do pretty much everything. The unconscious endocrine system decision-making that our body continuously does is far faster; it works in parallel with the rational part of our brains and often has a higher capacity, and is remarkably effective.

There are seven generally accepted primary feelings that we attach to the emotions arising in our bodies [19]. We can feel fear, contempt, disgust, sadness, anger, surprise, and joy. Different cultures describe them in slightly different ways, for example in the Chinese practice of Qi Gung grief is grouped with sadness, and worry replaces disgust. Notwithstanding these differences we can see that any of the many other feelings that we experience can be seen as a sub-set of these seven. Frustration for example is an aspect of anger, as happiness is a part of joy. It is interesting that the majority of feelings are what we might think of as negative and only one describes something positive, with surprise being contextual and capable of being either positive or negative.

Even the words themselves, emotion and feeling, can be problematic for many people in the workplace. In many of the workshops I facilitate I notice some participants 'close up' even at the mention of the word emotion or feeling. Their arms fold in front of them and they lean back, and some look away. I quickly learned that descriptions about our physiological reactions can help to explain what is going on if there is resistance. A scientific and evidenced based way of communicating works for people who are uncomfortable or unsure about feelings and emotions. Knowing how and why emotions arise in the body can help us to accept them as our body's' way of keeping us safe, harking back to a time when the rapid release of a hormone meant the difference between life and death. We have evolved beyond this necessity in many ways, however we retain the same limbic and endocrine systems we had millennia ago.

The part of our body that is in charge of our reactions is the oldest reptilian part of our brain rather than the newer and more sensible pre-frontal cortex. As we know our old friend the amygdala does the job of first responder, comparing any incoming information to past events, and if it doesn't like what it sees it will activate our bodies defence (endocrine and nervous) systems. The brain gives the amygdala a privileged position in being able to hijack our entire nervous system. It does this in milliseconds and it takes a while for our rational brains to catch up, kick in and work out if the threat is real or not. By then we will have hormones flooding our system, oxygen being diverted away from the brain, and our hearts racing to pump it quickly to our muscles.

What this means is that anyone making decisions under pressure has to contend with an emotional reaction that can work against rational thinking. When we are in these situations we can *feel* threatened even if the threat is for example another person's genuine enquiry or the establishing of important facts. We can feel angry if others respond in ways that seem unsupportive. Or we can worry about how our decision will be perceived by others.

In this way we can see how our emotions and the feelings that we associate with them can derail us and why we might prefer to keep emotions out of the workplace. The flip side is that when we handle our emotions and the feelings we associate with them well, relational and cognitive tasks such as listening, collaborating, thinking clearly, assessing a situation, and seeing the bigger picture become easier and enriched. We can get more done as we work with and through other people when we take emotions and feelings into account.

When we don't pay attention to our own emotions we may become constricted and even paralysed with inaction. As if that wasn't enough, to complicate this some of our psychological preferences then amplify and we can double down on, for example, being more competitive, overly focusing on detail, over-consulting with or avoiding others, and many more possible psychological stress adaptations that we all experience.

When we are in the tight grip of this type of reaction we can even unconsciously spread the emotion and trigger everyone else. We have all felt the tension in someone else even if it is not spoken, and if they have any sort of authority we may in turn feel a stirring of uncertainty. In times of crisis a leaders role is to radiate calm and assurance while simultaneously communicating a sense of urgency. A tricky double act.

Self-awareness and the awareness of others

emotional states and the feelings that are ascribed to them are crucial for the relational and decision-making aspects of leadership.

Dealing with our body's physiological reactions

Once we realise that we are in the grip of a rapid emotional reaction, what Steve Peters calls the amygdala hijack, there are some simple techniques that we can use to manage the reaction and regain self-control.

Our single objective during an amygdala hijack is to buy a bit of time to allow our pre-frontal cortex to catch up with whatever is going on and recover our rational decision-making capacity. To recover full capacity we need to restore a full oxygen flow to the brain and calm our body's excited nervous system.

To buy ourselves a bit of time, and to allow our pre-frontal cortex to catch up, what we can do is;

- o Breathe deeply and slowly through the nose into the lower stomach. This is the highest quality of breathing that we can do and it will re-oxygenate our system and most importantly our brain, in the fastest time possible. Furthermore, our nervous system will feel reassured and after only a few breaths we will slowly begin to relax and restore normal operation.
- o Ask a simple open question of those that we

are with to allow us to focus on our breathing and calming. Get other people talking for another minute or two. Say *"tell me more about…"*, *"explain how this would work"*, *"what do we need to understand more…"* Use the time to listen to their reply *and* to continue breathing well.

o Quickly scan our body and notice which of our muscles are tensing. We will be holding tension somewhere in our body when we are under pressure as part of our fight – flight - freeze mechanism. It might be our shoulders, our foreheads may be furrowed, or our jaws may be clenched. Wherever it is, once you notice it you can consciously soften and relax the muscles, releasing and letting go the tension. It also helps to shift your physical position by moving slightly, so that you can begin the body's process of moving the tension *through* and away. This will help to discharge the reaction more quickly. If circumstances allow find a private space and wave your arms around, twist, or do some squats. Feeling silly while you do this is optional. In the wild, animals will naturally shake their bodies after a fight or flight event to discharge any residual tension.

o We can simply say to ourselves *'What is my plan to solve this problem?'*. This automatically engages the rational thinking part of our

brain, which can accelerate us through the emotional reaction.
- Maybe the hardest way of dealing with a difficult reaction is to verbalise it and to give a voice to the feeling. Yet the act of naming the feeling is fantastically effective and helps to neutralize the worst effects of an amygdala hijack. At the same time it helps those around us to understand what is happening. Once named, the underlying emotion begins to unblock as it is no longer suppressed or held tightly inside of us. People often rally round in such situations. The trick here is to not act out or be the emotion; rather it is to state what is going on simply and as calmly as possible. *"I am feeling really angry that we are in this situation"*, or *"I am feeling very frustrated right now"*, or *"this is confusing for me and it's making me feel anxious"*. We are not saying this in an angry, or frustrated, or anxious, way. That would be acting out the emotion and is likely to make things worse, as others emotional reaction is triggered. We will build on this when we come to dealing with the emotions of other people.

◆

Using the transactional analysis model from the last

chapter, an expression I have used many times with clients is that their job as leader is to 'remain the adult in the room' at a time when others are unable to do this. This requires the effective self-managing skills of emotional literacy.

It is interesting to note that meditation, of which mindfulness is an example, has been proven to reduce the actual physical size of the amygdala and potentially lower the level of an amygdala reaction during negative processing (National Library of Medicine). *"The amygdala is physically smaller in the brains of meditators"* (Sara Lazar, assistant professor of psychiatry, Harvard Medical School) [20].

Navigating the emotions of a difficult discussion

We have looked at how to manage an amygdala hijack reaction in ourselves. What though, if we have to manage a difficult conversation and notice the reaction in someone else? We sometimes condemn those that flare up or break down quickly, and yet this is simply a reaction in someone that hasn't had the good fortune to learn how to deal with their own amygdala hijack.

There are some very practical and simple techniques to help people through their reaction so that we get the best out of them and reach the outcome that we want to.

In their book *Getting to Yes* [21], Stone, Fisher and Ury from the Harvard Negotiation project (HNP) researched and discovered the three dynamics that are in play when we are having a difficult conversation. A difficult conversation might be anything with some sort of conflict like a trade negotiation, a performance or misconduct discussion, a relationship breakdown, a supplier quality issue, a debrief about a poor judgement call, or simply an argument. It is any situation where people are likely to be feeling uncomfortable and nervous. They called these dynamics the three conversations.

Paying attention to all three conversations offers the best chance of reaching a good outcome for all. This means a win - win outcome rather than win - lose or worse, impasse and failure. The three conversations are:

The Reality conversation is the one that we probably already prepare for and begin our difficult conversations with. It is about what has happened and what the issue is, using evidence and the perspective that we have, how the issue has had an impact and how we might rectify it, where we go from here, and so on. We will often have an incomplete picture of the situation, which means that we will have our own version of the situation based on the information that we have. Hopefully we will listen well to each other's perspective or version of reality to enrich our view, and if after doing this we end up agreeing we won't need a difficult conversation. If however we don't reach agreement about what has happened a difficult conversation will be necessary, and the gap between perspectives is the area that we will need to focus on. We will all be used to having a reality conversation.

However, if this is the only conversation that takes place the chances of resistance and deeper conflict increase. One or both parties will likely feel worse than before.

The evidence from the HNP suggests that most people care about what they do, and we know that most of us set out to do a good job and are well intentioned.

The Identity conversation explicitly acknowledges that in a difficult conversation something important and fundamental will be at stake for both people. Something becomes at stake when the issue is connected with how we see ourselves – our sense of identity - and engaging with what this might be holds one of the keys to good outcomes.

When we perceive a threat to our sense of identity we can defend as if our lives depend on it, counter-attack with blame, and explode with anger or find solace in sarcasm and cruel wit. Or we may be paralysed by fear. We will most probably not be the adult in the room. As we know our psychological ego can be fragile.

For example, an expert will have at stake her or his reputation as a technical guru if a recommendation that they have made has gone wrong. A manager will have at stake his or her authority as a leader if they cannot handle a truculent and difficult member of the team. A trade union leader will have at stake her or his commitment to their members if they are seen to concede too much in a negotiation. A junior team member will have at stake their job security if even a simple mistake is made.

As part of managing a difficult conversation we can engage with the identity conversation and simply say, *"I know that this is important to you"* or similar. If you know enough about them you can add, *"you are the expert in this area and it can't feel great for this to have gone wrong"*, or whatever you understand might be at stake. If you get it wrong they will correct you. This small and yet powerful statement of empathy will go some way to providing a pathway for the other person into the conversation that you want to have. This simple human act starts to establish trust so that the other person is able to properly engage with what you want to say. Their own threatened nervous system reactions will begin to lose their intensity.

The Feelings conversation builds on the identity conversation and acknowledges that if something is at stake and has gone wrong, our bodies will be experiencing emotions that we might or might not have translated into feelings. It is the territory of EQ.

As we know when we perceive ourselves as

being under attack our bodies will run the fight - flight - freeze programme before we realise what is going on. With all of the physiological changes described earlier it is our rational thinking capacity that suffers. We simply lose the ability to think straight. A 2013 study by The National Library of Medicine [22] highlighted how in the instant that we perceive that we have been criticized, three areas in the brain experience a reduction in oxygen, and in particular that *"higher-order cognitive control functions were attenuated"*. To put it another way, when we criticize someone, we are in effect cognitively disabling aspects of their brain function for a short period of time. At the moment when we need someone to be fully engaged they can lose some of their thinking capacity. This is when someone might blurt something or cannot think of anything at all to say. They might go blank. Their internal mental chatter could take on a darker turn. Panic can set in. This is their chimp as described by Steve Peters, out of control.

We can build on our identity conversation empathetic statement and say something like, *"it looks like you are feeling angry?"* We call this naming the emotion. Put a name to whatever feeling you see in the other person. She or he will either agree and talk about it, or they will not.

If they do agree with you their emotion will begin to unblock and be out in the open, and a more real and healthy discussion can start to happen. In releasing an emotion it may of course get emotional, which can be uncomfortable simply because as humans we generally don't like to witness the suffering of others. Just allow a bit of time for the expression to take its course, understanding that it will dissipate and change into genuine dialogue. During this time, manage yourself well so that you avoid becoming triggered yourself.

If they don't engage with your naming what you see, you can make a decision. We want to respect someone not wishing to engage in the feelings conversation, and this is not therefore something to push. Instead, you can assess if you can still have a productive discussion even as there is a difficult emotional reaction going on. Is the other person remaining engaged and able to talk about what has happened, or is their level of reaction so strong that this is not possible? If your judgement call is that they are not able to engage as you wish them to offer a break to give them time to calm themselves, and to think about what they want to say. You could ask them what they need, such as a walk in the fresh air. Agree for how long a break is needed, which could be anything from ten minutes to a couple of days. Reconvene and then you start over.

When we plan for a difficult conversation the second and third conversations are not usually considered and yet they hold the keys to outcomes that leave everyone feeling as good as they can after a difficult episode. The HNP research highlights how even a small amount of empathy – the regard for others part of EQ - can transform anxiety and defensiveness into open and productive dialogue.

♦

With practice we can become deft and skilled at being aware of our and others' emotions and act in ways that demonstrate this. We can take feelings into account as we make and implement decisions, remembering too that our decisions include how we want to behave with other people. When someone says, "it doesn't feel right" we can pay attention to what their body's intelligence is saying, and help them to tease out why. The body is an incredible source of information that can add richness to our decision-making.

In his book *"The Advantage"* [23] Patrick Lencioni writes about the five dysfunctions of teams. One of the five dysfunctions he calls 'lack of conflict', meaning that the elephant in the room is not talked about. This is the one thing that everyone is thinking yet no one is saying. In Lencioni's model to get to the point where the elephant is talked about there needs to be a healthy level of trust. Another way to say this is that people won't speak up unless there is enough emotional and psychological safety in the room. The perception of threat needs to be low enough for someone to risk saying something controversial. How high or low enough this level of threat needs to be before we can take this risk will be different for reach of us. A suggestion that Lencioni makes is that to create trust the leader needs to go first with their own vulnerability, concerns, hopes and fears, and lean in to their own EQ and psychological maturity. Others will more than likely follow this lead. As intuitive leaders we willingly accept the responsibility for the climate that we create, and the culture that others will be able to thrive in (or not).

In this way EQ is fundamental to how leaders engage with those that disagree with them and allow space for challenge. The alternative is to be surrounded with people that just say yes, to avoid healthy conflict, and as a result squash any chance of becoming a high performing and effective team. The skill of remaining in constructive dialogue with those that oppose us is central to sustaining good outcomes on an ongoing basis and a barometer for mature leadership.

Trust is a magical intangible ingredient and takes repeated effort over time to build. It can cruelly slip away from us in seconds. By considering different perspectives and opinions, acknowledging differences, remaining in dialogue even when it gets hard, by expressing ourselves well cognitively and emotionally, and of course being competent in our job, we can continue building trust even with our opponents. This level of skill is available to us all.

"Between stimulus and response, there is a space. In that

space lies our freedom and power to choose our response. In our response lies growth and freedom."
- *Viktor E. Frankl*

SUMMARY

- Being able to work with our and others emotions rather than ignoring or suppressing them enables us to remain super-effective, especially when the heat is on. The parts of the brain responsible for our emotions and feelings are crucial for the way that we make decisions.

- Emotional intelligence is the ability to perceive, express, and manage emotions, in the self and in others. A leaders EQ is positively linked with psychological safety and trust building, which in turn generates engagement and commitment.

- Emotions are our body's raw data. Feelings are our brains interpretation of the data.

- Anyone making decisions under pressure has to contend with an emotional reaction that can work against rational thinking. This stems from the old, reptilian part of our brain.

- Our single objective during an amygdala hijack is to buy a bit of time to allow our pre-frontal cortex to catch up with whatever is going on and recover our rational decision-making capacity.

o Our job when others are in the grip of an amygdala reaction is to remain the adult in the room. We can pay attention to the reality, identity, and feelings conversations, and use proven practical skills to help people through these situations.

o The body is an incredible source of information that can add richness to our decision-making.

EXERCISES

1. Simply know that by increasing your level of self-awareness (chapter 3 and 4) you are also increasing your EQ. This is because you will be paying more attention to what you are doing, thinking, and feeling and gaining personal insights, and then using that information in helpful ways with those that you work and live with.

2. Think about how you perceive, express, and manage emotions in yourself and with others. From what you know of yourself, identify two or three relational strengths. We all have some! It could be listening, keeping focused on the group objective, maintaining eye contact, being supportive, or many more. Now choose three relational aspects of how you operate that you want to get better at. For example, it could be any from the list above, or understanding others, expressing your emotions, speaking more slowly, using your body language, and more. Talk it through with a trusted friend or colleague and get their perspective. This is your initial inventory, which is helpful for goal setting.

3. One by one focus on one aspect each month and pay attention to the behaviour. Use the daily 30-day habit building process in chapter 3 (reflection) to

help you to develop specific behaviours that over time will increase your level of EQ.

4. When you experience a feeling (stemming from your body's reaction) that is uncomfortable, and therefore merits some enquiry, do this,
   Name the emotion to yourself as best as you can - 'I'm feeling [sad, angry, joyful etc.] and I felt like [I was alone, I wanted to explode, get a hug etc.]'
   Identify the learning the experience holds for you – 'when I felt [sad, angry, joyful etc.] what I wish I had done was [take a breath, asked a question, told her/him/them how I was feeling etc.]
   Over time this will develop your skill in noticing what is going on with your feelings, such that you can articulate and work with them more easily.

5. Use the tactics for dealing with our body's physiological reactions in chapter 6.

6. Use the tactics for navigating the emotions of a difficult discussion in chapter 6.

These last two points will increase your EQ ability to self-regulate and express feelings, and to work with the feelings of other people.

SEVEN

WHAT DO YOU STAND FOR?

"Someone who stands for nothing will fall for anything."
- *Malcolm X*

This chapter asks what we have left to believe in and fall back on when all else fails. It is about the deepest of our roots; our values. The things that we will stand up for, even when it is difficult to do so or when it is unpopular. Because to not do so would be to betray the very essence of who we believe ourselves to be.

Then we will remind ourselves of how we are each one small part of a long chain of human lives that began long ago, that will continue to stretch into the future for countless generations to come. Taking this longitudinal view can help us as we grapple with day-to-day pressures and dramas, and as we make important decisions. It reminds us that we are connected with our past and our future, and that the decisions that we make today can have lasting effects for many years to come.

◆

Being the person that we want to be and leading others are easy when things are going well. The decisions we make seem to fall into place and get accepted. Our stakeholders are onside and they offer the benefit of the doubt. The market and broader context are amenable and full of the kind of opportunity that we are primed to take. We understand the system well and know which levers to pull to make it work, and the dials and forecasts are all pretty much heading in the right direction.

For some of us, for some of the time, this sometimes happens. For most of us the reality is usually very different. Being the best we can be in whatever endeavor we are involved in is often far from easy, especially when things are bumpy. Finding our flow can be hard as we try to make sense of whatever is going on around us, and chart a way forward that avoids the icebergs and gives us the chance to go again another day.

I worked with a group of pharmaceutical leaders throughout 2020 as they scrambled frantically to adjust to the chaotic covid crisis, as one by one the sacred cows of running things were sacrificed so that they could get done in a few short months what would normally take several years.

In the financial crisis of 2008 I was a commercial director in a professional services firm and that was hard enough, with twelve-month budget forecasting reduced first to three and then one month due to the terrifying level of uncertainty that we were working with.

Wherever you are and whatever it is that you do, dealing with crisis becomes a part of the deal as we take responsibility. Whether the scale is large or small, or what we are dealing with is systemic or relational, external or internal, when it all kicks off we have to respond. Sometimes we are the last person standing.

Fighting to remain grounded and effective when the going gets tough, all the while being pulled in every direction, is how we learn about our capacity and some important aspects of who we really are. Some of us are able to rise to the challenges we face, while others of us fall short and hopefully remain in the game to have another go.

This chapter is about what we have to fall back on when all around us people are losing their heads. We will ask what it is that we stand for, what our guiding principles as a person and a leader are, whatever the role that we have. Bill George [24] called this our true north, the part of ourselves that we can lean in to when it can seem that there is little else to grab a hold of. Being clear within ourselves about what we stand for enables us to make decisions even when we are under enormous pressure and in the midst of drama and even chaos.

When we are clear within ourselves we automatically become clearer for others. The people around us come to know what is tolerated and what is not. The red lines of our guiding principles can shine brightly in the dark, showing us the way forward.

In the 2008 crash Paul, our CEO, stated clearly that we would hold our pricing at a time when every competitor was slashing their rates in desperate attempts to generate cash flow. There was huge pressure to follow the market as sales-people and leaders chased impossible targets and consultants looked at large, gaping gaps in diaries. Clients grappled with their own rapidly diminishing budgets. No one knew up from down. We invested in relationships and played the long game, adjusting what we needed to keep everyone onside. This turned out to be a masterstroke as we recovered far faster than everyone else. Paul was rock solid in his position and he radiated calm and assurance, generating high levels of trust.

From the perspective of those that work with and for us, who crave certainty when it is impossible to offer such a thing, trust is built when our people know whom they are following. Even at the best of times they may ask, "why would I follow you?" and when times are challenging this question can make the difference between success and failure.

We were following Paul, who stood for his belief in the value of relationship as the primary way to create long-term success.

Our personal values make it clear what we stand for. Many of us will already be working with the values of our organization, and if we are fortunate we will agree with most if not all of them and maybe even believe in some of them too. They may engender feelings of commitment and passion within us, and even pride as they paint a picture of what we are about.

How many organizations values though languish tiredly on posters and pens, and shout quietly from web sites, gathering dust as just another part of corporate branding, and then get betrayed by behaviours that reveal who people really are?

We shall see that our own personal values on the other hand emerge from our lived and hard-won experiences. We can embody them as our very own and take them with us wherever we go.

Twenty odd years ago when I first explored my own values I worked with a firm that specialized in authentic business. One of the exercises involved the writing and repeated honing of a sentence that included our newly defined values, and then reading it out loud to each other in short and recurring pair sessions. As feedback was exchanged the sentence gradually became crisper and more impactful, our confidence in speaking it out loud growing with each exchange.

The final round, after multiple iterations, involved simply standing in front of each other and silently embodying our purpose and values. It was profound and moving. We learned that we could communicate what we stood for without words.

What we stand for already sits deeply inside of

us, cloaked in the significant experiences we have already lived. Our job is to discover our values, to give them heat, light and water and enable them to come alive. To do this, some reliving of our significant life experiences is necessary.

I have evolved the process through repeated client work, and share it with you now.

◆

We need to firstly acknowledge that this is a task to take our time with. We rarely, if ever, look at our history with as much attention as we are about to. To some of us this may feel indulgent, and who wants to spend their time dwelling on the past anyway? The answers to this question show up in my coaching practice every day, as clients realise that their past shows up in their present and will continue to influence their future. We have the choice, here before us right now, of how we can harness our biography to strengthen our sense of who we are, to enhance our impact, and to make clear our red lines.

If we are making the transition into the second half of our life this is the work of defining the nature of the person that we are becoming. Regardless of where we are with our adult development we can put a stake in the ground and say, this is who we are!

Step 1

Our first step is to create a visual timeline of our lives lived so far. The format is simple and the style is fluid, based around the straightforward idea of a lived experience being either positive or negative. We could choose to work with a horizontal (time) line across the middle of a large piece of paper with our positive life experiences above the line and the challenging ones below. Or some may prefer a winding river from top to bottom with positive experiences to the left of the river and challenging ones to the right. Time moves across the line or down the river so that our early experiences are at the beginning, and the most recent at the end in a chronological flow.

The task is simply to capture all of the significant moments of your life, positive and negative, by writing down on your timeline a headline of what the experience was and the year that it happened. Use a second sheet, and even a third if necessary. This is not to be rushed like the other tasks that we do, rather we can take all the time that we want to so that we immerse ourselves in our back-story. After all, who we are today is the sum total of what we have experienced. You may like to draw pictures and use photographs, and adorn the timeline in ways that are colourful and playful. Or not, preferring instead the simple power of words. The style is your own.

If it was a difficult experience one or two words or a simple image may be all that is necessary. No one is looking. The process is what is important. Do not, though, ignore what was significant even if it was painful. Include everything.

Step 2

Once you are done and if you feel comfortable, the next step is to tell the story of your life to a good friend or companion, family member, close colleague, or intimate partner, for an hour or so. All they will need are their ears, and if possible an open heart. For now they can silence their urge to speak. Working through your timeline talk about what happened and how it affected you, both what you are proud of and were great occasions, and your disappointments and humiliations. There may be moments of silence, as you remember and contemplate. Allow yourself to talk about yourself in ways that you may not have talked before.

Clients often say afterwards that they "had never told anyone this before", even decades after an event. In this way the telling of your story becomes a radical act and a moving experience as we acknowledge what has got us here, and how we have been forged by the white heat of life's tumults and celebrations.

Step 3

Next, we can begin the process of teasing out our values.

For each significant event above and below the line, or to the left and the right of our river, ask yourself the deceptively simple question *"what did I learn from this experience?"*

This form of reflection will cast each situation into the role of teacher, however difficult or brilliant it was. We can begin to understand that it is usually what was most difficult that holds the most learning. Success makes for poorer quality compost as we look to grow into the next version of who we are.

For example, an experience may have taught me to not trust those in authority. Or I learned that others sometimes can be genuinely kind. I may have learned the importance of preparing well and engaging with the detail. Perhaps I learned to manage my boundaries as it dawned on me that many people take more than they give. I may have learned that organizations can be dark places, full of ghosts and devils, or that speaking the truth is hard and yet ultimately all that we have. Perhaps I learned that I am not perfect, or I realised that I have to take responsibility for myself. And so on.

This step, again, will necessarily take time. Do your best to look at yourself with curiosity and kindness and avoid getting hooked into the drama of what has played out in the past. Honour the teachings. Make notes as you go.

Step 4

Once you have written your story and maybe told it to someone around a real or imagined campfire, and now that you have mined the experiences for the gold and diamonds of their learning, you are ready to look for the real gems.

Stepping back from the detail of your timeline now is the time to ask, how might something that happened years ago continue to drive you? Which of these learning's will you allow to continue influencing your attitude to this day? Which events seem to be most pivotal for you and continue to resonate within you? How do they help you to frame what you stand for?

Remember that there are no right answers to these questions, and that we are sifting and searching for what we regard as our red lines, for what we might write on our shield if we had to go into battle.

This is deep contemplative work. If you get stuck, ask the one who listened to you tell your story what themes they noticed.

Once we have some idea of what these drivers and patterns might be, we can start to name them.

In the naming of them our values must be positive, even though some of the events that inspired them were negative. We want to stand for rather than against something. The trick here is not to focus on the negative tactics that we use to ensure we don't re-experience something ("I will never trust what people say ever again") but to ask ourselves *"how did that experience shape my attitude in ways that are positive and helpful?"* We might say instead, "I will only ever speak the truth" or "I will rely upon my instincts as I choose whether to trust or not".

Some examples:

If we have been burned by duplicity and lies and learned to not trust, we can say that the value of truth or integrity lies within us.

If we had to not voice our opinions and to not offend, and learned to keep our opinions to ourselves, we can say that the value of freedom of speech defines who we are.

If we were bullied, the value of courage is in us.

If we endured the shame of failing at something and then learned to pay attention to the detail or to work harder, we can say that the value of conscientiousness is in us, or that humility now shapes who we are.

If we have allowed ourselves to luxuriate for too

long in the adoration of others and come to rely upon what they say, and learned the importance of self-esteem, we may have the value of trusting our own voice.

If we have got a big call wrong and learned how fickle others can be, we can say that the value of collaboration or listening well to others is ours.

We will end up with several positively framed words or short sentences, and these are your values. Ideally you will have at least three, and most likely no more than six.

Write them down and sit with them. Come back to them, and feel into their 'pull' for you. Ask yourself which of these words will you enlist to your aid in the future? Which values can you truly commit to? Are some aspirational and to be nurtured, or are they already burning brightly within you? Like supporting a sports team or having a close friend, once the commitment is made you will have to see it through and allow these values to speak for you. They will become a part of your identity, and will guide your decisions. Others will come to know you for them. Choose your values wisely and carefully.

Step 5

Once the rich creative work has been done, then

what to do with them?

To reach the point of feeling comfortable wearing our values, so that they gently shimmer in the background, we will need to embody them. To integrate them into our psyche if you will. This requires regular attention, albeit for only a few seconds or minutes each day.

If you have a mindfulness or meditation practice, using your imagination invite your values in for a minute or so each day, and visualise them seeping into your bones. Commit to them in your mind. Recall why they are each important for you. I spent over five years with this practice and still do from time to time, even twenty plus years and two evolutions of my values later.

You can write them down on a note and stick it to the bathroom mirror or the fridge so that you see them every morning. Write yourself a recurring diary entry to recall them as you begin your work.

If the opportunity arises in your work to voice them, take it. Not necessarily as a lofty statement of *"these are my values"* to which one or two eyebrows may be raised, more as a *"lets remind ourselves what's really important here in how we handle this"* kind of way. More assertively, if clear lines would be helpful, it can be powerful to say *"this is a red line for me"*. Others will get the message. A few words can say a vast amount.

Then, as they settle inside you, as well as talking the talk you will begin to walk the walk of your values. This need not be conscious or deliberate, and we probably don't wish it to be, as we will most likely become self-conscious and a little awkward. The embodiment of values happens as we use them in our day-to-day lives, accompanied by our ongoing mindful attention. After a while we will notice that they start to arise in our mind as decisions need to be made, and as we approach tricky or challenging situations.

When the heat is really on, and people are beginning to lose their heads, we can use our values to guide us as to what to do next. We can ask, *"What is the most [value] way of acting right now?"* or *"Out of all of these options which decision is most consistent with my values?"*

Every few years we can ask if they remain relevant, and if any adaptation is required to keep them alive. I have done this a few times. Several years ago I reflected deeply on my value of freedom. It was when the Me Too movement took off and I realised throughout that period that I hadn't paid enough attention to the responsibility that comes with freedom of speech. This was amplified by the explosion of social media and all of the abuse that comes with it. I chose to retain freedom of speech as a value with an enriched and broader sense of what it means for me in relation to others, and added a new fifth value, of respect for others. These two coexist with love, compassion, and truth, as my values, and are what I stand for.

We can use our values to achieve far more by doing a bit less, remembering that we have already lived the hard work of forging them and now simply welcome them as a vibrant part of our identity.

"Values are like fingerprints. Nobodies are the same, but you leave them all over everything that you do."
- *Elvis Presley*

The Seventh Generation

"The world is not ours to keep, we hold it in trust for future generations."
- *Kofi Annan*

When he said this Kofi Annan may have been inspired by the seventh-generation principle, an old (anywhere between 1150 and 1500 AD) Haudenosaunee idea that the decisions that we make today should result in a sustainable world seven generations into the future.

The great law of the Haudenosaunee Confederacy formed the social, political and ceremonial fabric of the original five nations of the United States of America. It is credited as being one of the main influences on the American constitution owing to founding father Benjamin Franklin's respect for the Haudenosaunee system of government.

As we make decisions that have implications for the future we can see that we have an invisible stakeholder, a group not yet born and yet who will inherit the legacy of our present day decisions and actions just as we have inherited the world as it is from past generations.

Just imagine if a representative from the future, one or two hundred years from now, could sit in on our present day decision-making discussions and have their voice heard and their welfare taken into account. How different do you think our decisions would be? It requires the kind of maturity that we have looked at in this book to take the long view and consider a time when we will be dust and a memory in the minds of our future families. Next generation leadership is what this maturity might look like.

Many decision makers and administrators will do and say anything to promote their interests. Even as we imagine ourselves to be well intentioned some of us allow ourselves to become compromised. Such is the nature of the systems that we operate in that in order to succeed we have to secure support from others, and sometimes we give a part of ourselves away in the process. We open ourselves up to lobbying, and to political and financial pressure from our sponsors. When this happens it is less likely that the welfare of even the next generation is factored into important decisions, let alone seven generations ahead. Their voices remain silent.

How then do we hear the voice of the seventh generation and allow it to influence decisions? In modern thriving nations this is a systemic issue, even as it is tempting to demonize specific people in the public eye. Because it is systemic the leaders that we so desperately need are those that will build better systems. Better political, economic, regulatory and social systems, with all of their associated processes for getting things done, so that we can hand on a way of life to future generations that is healthy, satisfying, and in balance for all beings on the planet.

Gaze out of your window for just a moment, and imagine what it would be like to be born into that kind of world.

What does it take to build better systems when we have seen that even in the face of overwhelming evidence that leaders continue to derail and delay what to most of us seems obvious and even inevitable?

We can each embark on perhaps the greatest act of innovation that we will ever do. We can do what we can to reach our own potential as fully functioning adults. To outgrow our old patterns, recognize our drivers and our shadows and ghosts, to imagine for ourselves how we want to be and how in our own way we can each contribute to building better systems. To change our own thinking so that we no longer approach problems with the same patterns that helped get us here in the first place. When we reach psychological and emotional maturity, we are nobody's fool, and not interested in fooling others. We are capable of doing amazing things.

This is radical work.

Once we have the opportunity for responsibility, to accept it in whatever form it takes. Large or small, across any sector in any walk of life, and with a good attitude.

As we engage with what needs to be done we can lead a dialogue about power and how it is held. We can ask for whose benefit power is conferred, and how it is to be used. We will understand what the responsibilities are that come with power, and to whom those in power are truly accountable including the seventh generation. We will demand that those with power meet us where we are.

Just imagine systems with full transparency of how key decisions are made, explaining how competing needs are balanced and why, and what the true costs in direct and indirect terms are of whatever is agreed. It is a system where the future is more important than the past, and where individual and collective needs are properly in balance.

It starts with imagination and vision and a conviction that we can do better. Then it becomes the hard work of converting vision into a reality that gets us closer to where we want and need to be.

Ultimately it is a leadership issue, because the far-reaching decisions with their ramifications echoing down the ages start with who is in the room making decisions.

Imagine leaders with a deep sense of awe and wonder as they contemplate the world that we live in, and an awareness of the needs of generations to come. These are people that have cultivated their wisdom. They have the competence and drive to outcompete those for whom the pursuit of power and material reward is the beginning and the end of their ambition.

These kinds of leaders rebuild antiquated, rusting and self-serving systems.

It is precisely what the world cries out for right now, across all sectors, regardless of how an organisation or body is funded, and regardless of geography.

No matter how big or how small our area of responsibility, whatever field of endeavor we are involved in, and wherever we operate, we each have a part that we can play. We cannot continue to leave it to other people. It starts with the self. If we were each to do this then the system would take care of itself, because we are all in effect 'the system'.

Let us act for our future generations. Let the seventh generation write a history that recognizes how we overcame present day challenges and honours those that stood up when they needed us to.

"Pull a thread here and you will find that it is attached to the rest of the world."

- *Nadeem Aslam.*

SUMMARY

- Being clear within ourselves about what we stand for and what we won't enables us to make decisions even when we are under enormous pressure and in the midst of drama and even chaos.

- It is our personal values that make it clear what we stand for.

- This clarity is very helpful for those around us. It helps others to understand what is important.

- What we stand for already sits deeply inside of us, cloaked in the significant experiences we have already lived. We can harness our biography to strengthen our sense of who we are, to enhance our impact, and to make clear our red lines.

- As we make decisions that have implications for the future, we can see that we have an invisible stakeholder, a group not yet born who will inherit the legacy of our present-day actions.

- Imagine leaders with a deep sense of awe and wonder as they contemplate the world that we live in, and an awareness of the needs of generations to come. These are people that have cultivated their wisdom. They have the competence and drive to outcompete those for whom the pursuit of power and material reward is the beginning and the end of their ambition.

- This leader could be you.

EXERCISES

Simply complete the values exercise outlined in this chapter.

EIGHT

CULTIVATING YOUR INNATE WISDOM

"Yesterday I was clever, so I wanted to change the world. Today I am wise, so I am changing myself."
- *Rumi*

This chapter is about wisdom, and how to cultivate and ground the innate wisdom that we all have simply by virtue of being human. We can borrow the concept of wisdom from philosophy, and explore what practical application it might have for us, before figuring out what steps we can take to actually develop our wisdom.

◆

Sheridan has sat with me in coaching for many years. She has great skills as a general counsel and as a leader, and has moved a few times to new organisations, each time taking on bigger roles. She now sits at the top of her functional area in a large, diverse organisation with broad governance and risk accountabilities, and with her team dispersed across all of East and West Europe, and North

America.

Recently she was involved in a complex transaction involving a potential change of ownership of the large partner based firm that she works for. There was a lot of pressure as powerful players tried to push through a deal, and she found herself at odds with some of her board level colleagues. In her view the possibility of landing a large personal windfall was becoming a distraction and getting in the way of clear thinking about the long-term interests of the organisation. As the board began to evaluate the offer on the table, Sheridan's choice was how to position herself to have the influence that she wanted using her unique legal oversight perspective. We talked it through together from every which way, exploring various questions such as *"what is really going on here?" "what does your instinct tell you?"* and *"how might you be wrong?"*

She was very fast and her thinking fell into place quickly. As crunch time arrived she simply named what she saw. Alongside what was certain she highlighted what was speculative and not what it might seem. She spoke clearly and authentically from the perspective of the many vested interests. She reminded the board of the advice they had offered to countless clients over many years, and of the values that together they had carefully crafted as a senior leadership group.

In other words she acted wisely and selflessly, and helped to make a decision that continued to secure the organisations future.

Wisdom is one of those words that bring to mind 'wizened' men and women, deep from our archetypal memory. We know it has been a quality, an idea, for well over two millennia as we contemplate the thinking and writing of Pythagoras, Plato, Socrates, Aristotle, and all of the great philosophers. Far more recently, wisdom is the first named of six 'virtues' identified in a 2004 meta-analysis of human strengths, alongside courage, humanity, justice, temperance, and transcendence. Christopher Peterson and Martin Seligman reviewed over 2,500 papers and worked with forty scholars in this monumental work, eventually publishing *Character Strengths and Virtues: A Handbook and Classification* [25].

What relevance does an essentially philosophical construct have to offer 21st century leadership and personal development thinking? I hope to make the point that it actually has quite a lot. A modern, practical and grounded application of wisdom, inspired by centuries of deep thought and discussion, is needed now perhaps more than ever.

The word philosophy actually means "the love of wisdom". Wisdom is variously described as "the ability to use your knowledge and experience to make good decisions and judgements" (Cambridge), "knowledge of what is true or right coupled with just judgement as to action: sagacity, discernment, or insight" (Collins), and "the quality of having experience, knowledge and good judgement" (Oxford).

Socrates talked (he famously never wrote anything down, believing writing to be an inferior method for inquiry; he left writing to his student Plato) about the humility of wisdom, Aristotle distinguished between theoretical and practical wisdom, and the Chinese traditions, including Confucian, gravitated towards an interpersonal interpretation, for example the 'speaking of knowledge'.

If we take a hawk's eye meta-view of wisdom material and look for consistent themes from across the ages, we can see that five distinct skills begin to emerge that have real contemporary relevance and a valuable place in personal and leadership development.

These "five practical skills of wisdom" are:

Being able to really see what is going on from multiple perspectives

Buddhism calls this "a penetrating way of seeing" and it requires the ability to see things simultaneously for context, and with a laser focus on specifics.

This way of seeing with breadth and depth, or of seeing around corners as opposed to working with what is right in front of us, enables us to 'cut to the chase'. It goes beyond big picture or strategic thinking. When we see in this way we use our ability to sift what is relevant, quickly identifying and disregarding what is irrelevant. Acting wisely requires paying attention to many types of information; facts and data, social and political context, relational factors at individual and group levels, past and future, and what might be half-hidden at the edges of our awareness. Otto Scharmer in his work *Theory U* [26] suggests that when we are analysing a situation, that we take perspectives from the margins of whatever systems that we are in, and encourages speaking with those that others may ignore.

The skill of seeing in this way is based on an all-encompassing intelligence that includes but is not limited to conventional cognition. From a modern point of view we could say that all of our senses are in play including our intuition and gut instinct, in a 'whole body' way of seeing and sensing. We know from neuroscience research that in addition to the brain, the heart and the gut have their own systems of neurons that fire rapidly in ways that we don't properly comprehend. How we understand the very nature of our intelligence, and where our intuition might come from, is adapting and changing as we research and continue to learn.

When we think of using the self, including our intuition, as a tool for change we will utilize our experiences and memories to inform, or see, a present day dilemma with possible future implications. It is our learning from the past and ability to map present situations to it that enables this penetrating way of seeing, as well as our trust in the various forms of intelligence that we have available to us.

To act wisely we will have done our ten thousand hours of live practice, Malcolm Gladwells suggestion for how we acquire mastery, and have rich memory banks to source our insights from.

Good decision making

This has been called "right judgement" and is essentially how our "penetrating way of seeing" is used. With wisdom we are able to think and intuit pathways forward that advance things with clear recommendations or firm decisions. As we shall see in (3) decisions made are for the benefit of the collective and the whole system (pro-socially) rather than only for personal gain or narrow self-interest. We can see how decision-making from a conventional psychological adult maturity position might be very different from a post-conventional position, and that the deeper into adult psychological maturity one gets the broader the level of 'felt' accountability to others become.

When we make wise decisions we will not be concerned with 'being right' with our decisions but to help to get to the right answer, even if this means giving ground to others or ceding the limelight. This detachment from our ego need to be the hero that has solved the problem frees up the whole psyche in service of whatever is going on, enabling a more creative and balanced way to make 'right judgements'. In this way there are no games being played, no power plays, and an absence of the drama that we can get lost in.

As we apply learning from the past to present situations, we avoid history repeating itself over and over unless this is our conscious choice. As we do this good decision-making becomes wisdom in action.

Guided by clear values

Even if we see things clearly from multiple perspectives and use what we see to make sound decisions, those decisions can still create exclusion and division. Of course, not everyone will agree with wise decisions and there is often opposition and challenge. In thriving environments this is to be welcomed. While disagreement can feel uncomfortable however it need not derail what is necessary. What helps others to accept decisions that they disagree with is that they will have had the opportunity to discuss and engage, and others will know and trust what decision-makers stand for. Wise decision makers will change their position as new information comes to light, and as new perspectives are discovered.

'Doing the right thing' (applying right judgement) is guided by pro-social values. These values acknowledge that the bigger picture is often more important than individual needs. This is about the balancing and prioritising of needs between the collective and individuals. Acting wisely prioritises for the greater good, which we have seen in chapter 7 will include future generations. An attitude of benevolence is central to modern wisdom thinking.

To flip it around, a decision that is designed to serve the self and those that are close and only of the same 'tribe' cannot be a wise decision if it comes at the expense of others. A 'right' decision that satisfies economic, political, or social pressures may not be a wise decision. Climate emergency decision-making is an example of this as we inch rather than race forward with vital action.

By acting with wisdom we acknowledge how decisions have different impacts on different groups. We are open with information and give a voice to those in disagreement, partly in service to consensus and also as disagreement often contains useful information.

In classical writing, wisdom values include having 'good conduct' (biblical), compassion (Buddhism), and 'courage to act' (Aristotle). Wisdom has been described as *"any factor that facilitates a greater positive engagement with the whole"*, (Attlee 2004) meaning pro-social engagement with the collective alongside the needs of the individual. We could add values such as humility, freedom of thought, transparency, and benevolence. These values are compatible with a modern, thriving, commercially oriented way of life, and do not get in the way of us being clear, smart, driven, and assertive.

In chapter 7 each of us will have worked out what we stand for. Our work is to be clear about what values guide us, and to cultivate our own wisdom.

Acknowledging uncertainty

Socrates said, *"The only true wisdom is in knowing you know nothing"*. With wisdom we become aware of what we don't know, and acknowledge the inherent mystery of life.

Living with ambiguity and not knowing seems to be a fundamental and almost existential collective modern-day challenge as we try to make sense of what is going on. We have access to more information from many more sources than ever before, quite literally at our fingertips, and yet with less trust than ever in the truth of what we read. For our psychological safety our brains prefer complete stories rather than be left with unfinished business, such that many of us would prefer inaccuracy and even conspiracy to the psychological threat of not knowing what is going on. We mis-read in to situations, not believing what we are told by authorities (often appropriately), and default to the assumption that others have it in for us (paranoia) as opposed to assuming that others have our best interests at heart (pronoia). We are left with the paradox that the more that we know and discover, the more that we see what we don't know.

Sitting comfortably with ambiguity and uncertainty becomes very necessary for our mental health and sense of well-being, as well as for how we cultivate our wisdom.

Thus to Socrates we can humbly add knowing that there are things that we don't know that we don't know, with acknowledgement to Donald Rumsfeld as well as the pioneers of the 'Johari window' [27]. The latter is a helpful model from 1955 that categorises self-awareness into the four quad-rants of what we know (the open window), what we choose to not disclose to others (the hidden window), what we do not see in ourselves yet others do (the blind window), and what we are all unconscious to (the unknown window).

Philosophy offers a fifth perspective of the unknown knowns, or that which we choose to not acknowledge; that which we do not like that we know. For example, in many countries arms and defence industry sales generate unbelievable levels of revenue and tax income, and in highly important respects keep us safe. As we sell them we know that they are likely to be used at some point and that we will therefore be able sell more in the future, securing a long term revenue source. However, we choose to not openly acknowledge the death, pain and destruction that our arms sales are guaranteed to cause to fellow human beings, usually many miles away from us. We prefer these realities to be out of our sight and therefore out of our mind.

No matter how difficult it is wise to engage with all perspectives and see things for what they are, and to be aware that there are likely to be things that we do not like that we see.

The humility that comes from acknowledging that we can't know everything, when combined with our conviction and our values, fuels a compelling and wise leadership voice. It helps us to avoid the fevered certainty that blinds us to options and possibilities. It infuses and flavours our communication so that those around us can feel more comfortable with their not knowing.

Wise people sometimes reply 'maybe' when others have certainty of right and wrong, because they know that we don't always really know.

Taking time for reflection

We know that reflecting helps us to learn from our experiences, and builds our sense of what we stand for and our personal values. This is in itself wise action.

The humility stemming from (4) above is often acquired through experiencing our own personal challenges and failures and then reflecting on them. The acquisition of the feeling of invincibility that we do in our younger lives, as we look to establish and strengthen our ego identity, gets us ahead of our competitors yet does nothing to develop our humility. The opposite in fact, as the absence of humility from strength becomes arrogant and unyielding, leaving others with no room or space to participate.

Those acting with wisdom will almost certainly have experienced pain and maybe even suffering, as we all do. The wisdom stemming from reflecting on these experiences will show up in decisions as right judgement. This reflection also delivers the rich insight and learning that inform and shape who we are. Our own life experience then becomes one of the central perspectives in (1) above. Even those that may be considered wise will continue to reflect regularly as a matter of course.

By reflecting on and learning from life's experiences we notice patterns and avoid repeating mistakes by applying what we have learned. History repeats through this lack of honest reflection. How often can we see disasters looming and yet still avoid the actions needed to avert them? It doesn't have to be this way.

We can use the reflection skills already described in chapter 3.

♦

These five wisdom characteristics can also be found

in a 7-component model created by the University of San Diego. The Jeste-Thomas Wisdom Index [28] comprises; acceptance of diverse perspectives, decisiveness, emotional regulation, pro-social behaviours, self-reflection, social advising, and to a lesser degree spirituality.

The potent blend of the five wisdom skills and attitudes characterises our own innate wisdom. As we have seen, at least in the way that wisdom is distilled to clear actionable skills, wisdom can be acquired through effort and intentional development. Each of us has the capacity and potential to *act* wisely, meaning that we can work with these five wisdom characteristics. We all have the potential to make choices and decisions that are wise. None of us is unable to act wisely. In this sense our wisdom is innate, in that simply by virtue of being human we have the seeds of wisdom within us.

It is, of course, for many of us latent. Not for nothing are the wisdom teeth so named, as they are the last to grow. This latency may remain for our entire lifetime, and perhaps it only properly flowers in those that have been moved to enter the second half of their psychological lives, from conventional and 'me' focus to post-conventional with all of the attendant collective attitudes.

Wisdom is different to IQ and traditional understandings of intelligence. It is not knowledge, which we can learn and acquire through reading and studying. Wisdom cannot be learned from a book even as it is one of the most written about topics that we have, in philosophy, religion and fiction. By consciously working with the five skills of wisdom we can reach the point where we are not even thinking about 'acting wisely', we simply act, and allow others to consider if we have acted wisely.

Perhaps in this age we have a general wisdom deficit, even though we are better educated than at any time in history. Maybe we always have had such a deficit and I am now noticing it more as I get older. As we have access to more information than ever before why do we keep making the same mistakes? How can we build systems that are inherently wise; able to apply what we learn from our and others experience while innovating and remaining open to new ideas and resources, like a human version of machine learning?

Jung wrote about collective psychological dynamics in *The Undiscovered Self* [29] and identified the necessity for serious individual development work as a precursor to collective work. This book calls for the same.

Wisdom, elders and mentors

"They say I gotta learn, but nobody's here to teach me."
- Coolio, *Gangsta's Paradise*

Elders have had roles in societies and communities ever since there were groups of humans living together. These were, and still are in some communities, those wise folk that carry community (collective) responsibilities and are consulted when important decisions need to be made.

In African tribal societies elders were praised as 'transmitters of culture and carriers of tradition', and as 'guardians of the secrets of life'. They were sometimes referred to as 'The Wise', people to consult with in avoiding conflict and preserving peace.

In Aboriginal culture those older people that have the title elder conferred on them have years of service to their communities, and carry a big responsibility to pass on stories of the past that help the growth and development of the next generations.

One modern way in which the essence of eldership is used is in the practice of mentoring. The 'wise counsel' who has already trod the path being taken. Mentors are sometimes called 'professional friends', and with good reason.

Mentors talk about their own experience with regard to whatever topic the 'mentee' brings in to the conversation, and consequently are required to have experience with the context, technicalities, and challenges faced by those they work with. They will disclose what they, too, found difficult, and how they overcame their difficulties. There may be suggestions, and there will certainly be ideas shared. The mentor will look to expand the range of perspectives of the mentee, much like in coaching.

The words coaching and mentoring are sometimes used interchangeably, although there are subtle differences around style and approach with probably less storytelling in coaching. Furthermore, coaches do not need, per se, knowledge of the technicalities and direct experience of the challenges faced by those they work with. Where coaching and mentoring overlap however is in the aim of both to become places of learning. Not so much of telling and direction as ultimately we all have to find our own way through the dark woods, but if someone is able to shine a bit of a light on what we are dealing with and highlight the tree roots on the path then this can only help.

Mentoring becomes a way in which an individual with hard won experience is able to hand something on to the next generation, in the way that many of us benefited from something similar when we were younger and just starting out.

Just imagine if we all had access to objective elders or mentors, with whom we could get unvarnished and apolitical points of view from wise people that have the psychological and emotional maturity to not get drawn into the drama or vested interests of the situation.

Non-executive directors, advisory committees, charity board members, and the like, all have the potential to fulfill the wisdom role of eldership for those that they serve. For sound governance reasons most of these bodies have their roles well defined, often legally as in the case of boards. When this happens it is easy for the formal role to get in the way of the adding of real value. Legal obligations do not always add up to serving the real needs of the host organization.

I worked with the CEO of a large and successful charity in the UK, with a well meaning but utterly draining board of trustees so consumed with oversight that they forgot to allow any space for the executive of the charity to flourish, so suffocating were they.

Arnold Mindell is a process psychologist and author of many books, as well as an acknowledged expert in conflict resolution. He has worked with conflict at the level of nations. In his book *The Leader as Martial Artist* [30] he outlines a view of leadership, and most interestingly goes on to contrast leadership with a contemporary view of eldership. We might say it is an idea of what wise and mature leadership looks like. It is unashamedly broad, and much like the material in this book he draws from both mainstream and non-mainstream thinking. Mindell writes;

"The leader follows Robert's Rules of Order*, the elder obeys the spirit.

The leader seeks a majority, the elder stands for everyone.

The leader see trouble and tries to stop it, the elder sees the troublemaker as a possible teacher.

The leader strives to be honest; the elder sees the truth in everything.

The democratic leader supports democracy; the elder does this too but also listens to dictators and slaves.

Leaders try to be better at their jobs; elders try to get others to become elders.

Leaders try to be wise; elders have no mind of their own, they follow the events of nature. The leader knows; the elder learns.

The leader needs a strategy; the elder studies the moment.

The leader follows a plan; the elder honours the direction of a mysterious and unknown river."

---

*In the United States *Roberts Rules* were created to provide a consistent approach to governance, and as such are heavy on process and light on wise counsel and engagement for all but the most compliance minded. They have however heavily influenced leadership in the US at all level of society, even as they come to be questioned as out of touch and out of date. They are used in more authorities, councils, and bodies than any other form of guidance for governance in the US.

◆

There is much to unpack in this. Some of the underlying ideas come from meta-physics and spirituality. The language is poetic and to some it will seem idealistic. It may resonate more with someone in the second half of their psychological life who is very comfortable in their not knowing, and in their reliance on feedback 'from the system' (whatever is happening around them in the moment) to guide and inform how they act or don't act.

For these people, these wise elder mentors, their wisdom is not their own it seems but that of the world around them. It is a collective wisdom that is available to all of us, perhaps in the vein of Jung's collective unconscious. They will have reached the point of letting go of their own wisdom, which in itself will have been accrued over many years, and instead to rely on their connection with the essence of life itself to provide whatever answers will serve whatever needs to be served. This idea may trouble those that rely on materialist thinking and an evidence base before they can take on board and commit to new ideas. What we are doing here is pushing at the limits of the current way of thinking and adding to the way that we make decisions. No one can say that the current systems are working so well and meeting the needs of the collective, after all. Perhaps a place to start is to focus on the grounded skills of wisdom, and to let the rest take care of itself.

If eldership does find you, wear this particular coat of many colours well. Many will be served by your involvement.

"Life can only be understood backwards; but it must be lived forwards."

- *Soren Kierkegaard*

SUMMARY

- Wisdom comprises five distinct skills that have contemporary relevance and a valuable place in personal and leadership development.

- It is our learning from the past and ability to map present situations to it that enables our 'penetrating way of seeing'.

- When we act wisely we are not concerned with 'being right' but to help to get to the right answer, even if this means giving ground to others or ceding the limelight.

- The humility that comes from acknowledging that we can't know everything, when combined with our conviction and our values, fuels a compelling and wise leadership voice.

- By reflecting on and learning from life's experiences we notice patterns and avoid repeating mistakes by applying what we have learned.

- Our wisdom is innate, in that simply by

virtue of being human we have the seeds of wisdom within us. We can cultivate and develop our ability to act wisely.

o Mentoring is a way in which an individual with hard won experience can use their wisdom and hand something on to the next generation.

EXERCISES

1. Bring to mind a tricky situation that is current, or at least very recent, and develop a penetrating way of seeing by consciously taking at least four or five different perspectives on what is going on. Look at the situation through the eyes of others, even (particularly with!) those you disagree with or may have dismissed as unimportant. Have a deliberately curious attitude and an open, detached mind. Notice your own assumptions about the people involved and what is going on, and ask yourself if these assumptions are true. Ask yourself what this situation reminds you of from your past, and take any learning from that reminder. Imagine what someone brand new to the situation would have to say. Identify the 'elephants in the room' and what others are afraid to talk about.

2. Develop good decision-making by creating options and evaluating the impact on all of those with a vested interest, however marginal, and including future generations (see chapter 7). Be clear about the difference between self-interest and collective interest, and whom each option serves the most. Ask how the decision will serve those who will live with the decision after you have left. Notice what you are afraid of as you contemplate the

decision. Pay attention to your instincts and notice what you are naturally drawn to and repelled by. Ask how consistent your preferred option is with your personal values and what you stand for.

3. Do the work of clarifying what you stand for (chapter 7), and ensure that at least two of your values are pro-social.

4. Develop your relationship with uncertainty and not knowing by working with the Johari Window framework as you think about the situation. Talk it through with colleagues or friends and compare what you don't know. Be clear about the difference between facts and opinions, and how complete a factual portrayal actually is. Understand what is verifiable and what isn't, including what might be 'received wisdom' or an outdated assumption. Openly talk about what is not clear and hidden from view, so that others have permission to do the same.

5. However you engage with the inherent mystery and wonder of life – gazing at the stars, sitting in nature, reflecting on thousands of years of humanity, being with young children or those at the end of life – acknowledge that there is much that we don't, and won't be able to, understand. Use this perspective to get comfortable with any present-day uncertainty.

6. Develop your ability and capacity to reflect by working with the ideas in chapter 3.

Finally…
7. If you are invited to become a mentor, take it. The world needs more mentors.

NINE

CHANGE AGENCY FOR THE SELF

"If you do not change direction, you may end up where you are heading."

- *Lao Tzu*

This chapter is about the enablement of ourselves, and how to make sure that we can achieve what we set out to as we plan our psychological and emotional development. It would be great to think that this journey will be all plain sailing; the reality however is that development can sometimes be difficult. Understanding what is going on as we plan and take steps to develop ourselves can help us to put ourselves in a strong position to get change to stick. In this way, we will be far more likely to reach our goals.

◆

John was frustrated. He was eighteen months in to his role with a new company and had established a great reputation by cranking through large volumes of work at a high level of quality, while building excellent relationships with his stakeholders. He'd also made some long overdue changes to his team, showing leadership and clear thinking about his area of the operation.

We had talked a few times about shifting the balance between the time he spent on day-to-day operational work and the broader strategic goals he shared with his boss. With what needed to be done his aim was to get the latter to around twenty percent, effectively one day a week, which given the work volumes he was getting through meant delegating more to his team to free up some time.

He was frustrated because he had tried the usual tactics and hacks that we work with to manage his time better, yet he couldn't make the shift in balance that he wanted. His boss was starting to get impatient as the broader agenda for the function was becoming compromised. We used the coaching space to explore what was going on, and how it was that John was somehow getting in his own way.

He sat back and smiled at the light bulb moment. By changing his working pattern such that he would spend less time with his clients, he realised that the resulting threat to his painstakingly built reputation for being 'the guy' for his clients was far stronger than he thought it was. In effect he was asking himself to reign in the very thing that he had done to establish his reputation, even as this was necessary for him personally and for the business. This wasn't a conscious weighing up of pros and cons; it was his unconscious tricking him into doing just one more piece of client work before starting the strategic work. And then that other priority for a colleague, until the time allocated had gone and he was back into the flow of his daily schedule. The deeper drives of his psyche had been in charge all along.

This 'naming the monster' as John came to call it was a pivotal moment. He now knew what he was dealing with, and he could begin to have a different conversation with himself as it came to using his time, as well as making time to communicate with his stakeholders and explain what was going on. His insight provided the fuel to change what he wanted and he quickly got back on track with his strategic work.

Changing is hard for many reasons and perhaps none more so than the fear of letting go of safety, even if it no longer serves us.

Some years ago I came across the work of Robert Kegan and his book *Immunity to Change* [31], written with Lisa Lahey. The material is based around Kegan's adult developmental psychology research at the Harvard Graduate School of Education. He had come across the astonishing fact that only one out of seven seriously ill heart patients in the US make the necessary changes to their lifestyle that would keep them alive, even with all of the information in front of them. Many do not even take their medications. This change resistance research has enormous applicability for personal and leadership development, and I often use his findings and insights in my coaching practice, much like with John.

So, what is going on? Kegan and Lahey dug deeply into the human psyche to answer this question. They went beyond the usual development language of goals and milestones, SMART actions, support and motivation, helpful though these are as we shall see later.

Their work led to the insight that if we are being asked to change something about how we operate, then the outcome will in some way reshape our sense of who we are. As well as this reshaping being positive, it can also trigger our unconscious psychological threat response. A change to the way that we operate can *appear* as threatening to our complex psychological identity even if it is what we need and something that we have initiated. This instinct for safety and familiarity is so strong it will stop us doing what we need to do. We will continue drinking beer with our friends in our favourite bar even as we know it will be bad for us, because of an unconscious assumption that we would be ejected from our social group if we didn't. Or as a leader at work we might avoid endorsing the party line or even criticise a decision that we don't agree with, as it might alienate us from people that work for us and get in the way of our seeing ourselves as 'one of the guys'.

This is quite profound; this acknowledgement

that we have such strong drives within us for social belonging, status, or reputation for example, that they work at the expense of our goals and for some our personal health. We are indeed a complex species. Kegan and Lahey called these drives our *Hidden Competing Commitments*. For every goal that we set for ourselves we are likely to have buried needs that feed off keeping things just as they are. These drives and impulses include the same psychological needs we have discussed already; for control, approval, and security and our fear of losing them.

They go on to describe how at the heart of these hidden competing commitments are one or two big *Assumptions* that we hold about these needs, and these unconscious assumptions are what we need to understand if we are stuck. For example,

"If I stop [doing xxxx] my unconscious will assume that my reputation / success / status / financial security / lifestyle / way of working etc., will be threatened and…

…I will be ejected from the group / disrespected / marginalized / humiliated / sacked / fail etc."

The reality is that the fear behind our assumptions is almost always way out of proportion to the actual level of risk of these things happening. Our threat response is, once again, in overdrive.

John assumed that his fantastic reputation with

Partners would be damaged if he didn't personally deliver an outstanding and responsive service to them, even as he built a capable team around him. His unconscious assumption was *"they know me for doing this work, and if I don't do it they won't value me any more"*. His fear was disapproval. This took the energy out of his efforts to step back from the day-to-day and spend some time on longer-term strategic work.

In many years helping clients with their development it has become clear that it is the stopping doing rather than the starting doing that is usually the most difficult. The unlearning of our ingrained patterns requires so much more effort than learning something new. Changing some aspects of what got us here, as we know, requires effort and commitment.

The reflective inner work that throws a light onto these aspects of our psychology takes us to a deep level of self-awareness from which we can manage a healthier internal dialogue and make better quality decisions. It is only by revealing our hidden competing commitments and underlying assumptions that we can see them for what they are and move forward cleanly. All the while that they remain in our unconscious they will tick away, sabotaging our best hopes for ourselves.

As we contemplate the transition from the first to the second half of our psychological life, we can begin to understand why it can be such a difficult phase for us to navigate. Perhaps at this threshold more than any other what we think, what we believe, and what we assume, are all being questioned. As we won't yet have worked out any answers to these questions it is perfectly understandable that we will hold on to our 'old selves' with a tight grip. Not letting go offers certainty, even as we also feel that our skin is inexorably shedding.

Using mystical and even existential language, and to consider change from the perspective of the ego, to change something of who we are is to accept that a part of our old identity will have to die. It sounds dramatic doesn't it, and yet those hidden competing commitments and assumptions that we have nurtured over decades, and that we have now elected to leave behind, have woven themselves more deeply into our psyche than we might have thought. The process of unlearning and release carry a price. We have unconsciously identified with them, and as we let them go our ego identity will, for a short time at least, feel the poorer for it.

Change can be scary.

Don't wait

Imagine canyoning down a steep mountain, tracking a small river through a series of deep plunge pools. Hemmed in as we are to the landscape, we cannot see the pool that we have to jump into from what seems to be a terrifying height.

We jump into the void anyway, hearts thumping, waiting for the cold water to affirm life.

There will come a moment in changing where we simply have to jump or let go despite our fear, rather than waiting until we stop feeling frightened, or threatened, for we probably never will.

It is these liminal moments 'in between' where the growth first takes root. We have made the commitment, taken the deep breath, and jumped. Well done us! The growth has taken root but a part of us may question if it will flourish. The new attitudes, behaviours, beliefs, skills, and patterns are yet to form, and so for a short while we are on shaky ground, coming to terms with how it feels. We have put on the new clothes and we are not sure if they really fit.

These are the moments when memories of the past appear to offer false comfort and certainty. What we are trying to unlearn appears as a ghost, wooing and seducing us.

Perhaps if I just told others what to do again it wouldn't hurt? It used to work didn't it? People did what they were told to do?

My outbursts, the uncontrolled explosions of anger, got things moving and everyone knew where they were?

Maybe I can continue to manoeuvre and manipulate behind the scenes so that I have the advantage when it comes to promotion time, after all everyone else does.

Withholding important information just once more won't hurt, after all it is how I have wielded power in the past and reached the level I am at now.

It will feel uncomfortable and awkward at first using new skills or ways of thinking. This could be as simple as asking a question and then trying to listen to the answer without interrupting. Or when we imagine what it is to walk in the shoes of others for the first time, or to promote their reputation rather than our own. Our ExCom colleagues may be surprised and a little wary as we no longer fight with aggression for control of scarce resources. Think back to your driving test and remember how hard you had to concentrate, and that you only really starting getting good at driving once you had passed.

Over time and with effort we will form new patterns and develop mastery over new skills. Our sense of our identity will evolve as we grow and expand, and we can know that we have matured.

The science of change

There is a fair amount of research about how long it takes to create new patterns. A UCL study by health psychologist Phillippa Lally [32] found that it takes at least two months for new behaviours to become automatic, and anything up to eight months depending on the complexity and frequency of use of the behaviour.

Research from neuroscience, and specifically the process of neuro-plasticity, helps us to go some way to understanding what is happening in our brains as we develop and change. Neuro-genesis is the constant production and integration of new neural pathways that takes place throughout our lives. This happens with all of us, all of the time. When we are very young we form over one million neural pathways *each second.*

Structural neuro-plasticity is the strengthening of these neural pathways, while functional neuro-plasticity describes the permanent changes to our synapses arising from our learning and development (Demarin, Morovic and Bene 2014 [33]). Synapses enable messaging between our brains neurons. In this way we experience a rewiring of our brains as we adapt to new circumstances. This is possible right up to old age, although the process slows down over time.

There are many variables likely to influence how long the functional neuro-plasticity rewiring process takes; the nature and complexity of the change that we are making, our age and attitude, our genetic profile, how much of and the nature of the support that we have around us, and the context and environment all have a bearing. It is in the early stages of functional neuro-plasticity that we are likely to be feeling less confident in how we apply what we are learning, as our brain adaptations are incomplete.

As we develop we firstly experience unconscious incompetence (I don't know what I don't know), before we move into conscious incompetence (I recognise that I'm not very good at something), and then conscious competence (I can do it but its awkward and hard work), before we habituate and embed our learning and move into where we want to be with unconscious competence (I can do it without thinking too much) (*The four stages of competence, Broadwell, Curtis and Warren 1960* [34]).

Positivepsychology.com make an interesting connection between neuro-plasticity and growth mindset, Carol Dwecks [35] work on the importance of our attitude to the achievement of learning outcomes. At a headline level, her work led to the insight that a growth (open) mindset attitude of positive expectations and willingness to learn from challenges leads to better learning outcomes than a fixed (closed) mindset attitude of resistance to change and a belief in innate qualities that do not shift over time. The connection between our attitude and our functional neuro-plasticity makes sense, and we can look forward to more research and evidence to support the hypothesis. In the meantime, there are enough case studies to state with confidence that adopting a growth mindset will help make change stick better than a fixed mindset. At the very least a growth mindset will help us to push through the stages of conscious incompetence and unconscious competence rather than give up when it gets hard.

Being aware that change is a process that can take time, and that these physical changes to our brains are happening as we learn helps us to accept the transition through change. In this way what takes root in us as we jump or let go is more likely to flourish.

Six proven tips for making change stick

These psychological and physiological characterristics sit alongside some practical and simple suggestions for making change stick. Start with these, and know that they will increase the chances of you getting to where you want to go.

Set a development goal
Probably the most important single thing that we can is to get really clear about the change that we want to make. We want this to be crisp, specific, and well-defined. We also want it to be realistic. Maybe further ahead we can think about being able to hold the attention of an enormous room of people for an hour, however in the short term it may be more than enough to successfully deliver a ten-minute session to a small group of colleagues.

Our goal can either be about 'content', meaning that it is skill based and something that we do, for example, to be more assertive with our peers, which will require changes to how we talk, our body language, and the words that we use. It may be to see the bigger picture more clearly from different points of view as we cultivate our wisdom.

Or our goal can be about 'context', meaning about who we are as people. For example, we may firstly wish to know what we stand for by reflecting on our biography, and then secondly to integrate what we learn into our leadership identity. Or we might want to know what our current level of psychological adult maturity is.

Some goals may be about both content and context. For example, to develop consistent and authentic assertiveness we will want to know what skills are required and to practice them, and also to understand where our lack of assertiveness (our aggression or passivity) comes from in our past, as we weren't born lacking assertiveness as any new parent will tell you.

For more complicated goals it is helpful to set interim milestones that build towards our ultimate goal so that we can be sure that we are making progress and on the right track. In this way we would break a six-month goal down into two or three interim milestones that once achieved will confirm, or not, that we are heading in the right direction.

Set a measure of success

This adds another layer of specificity to our goal setting. To do this we ask ourselves the important question, how we will know when we have reached our goal?

For a content skill-related goal we can look for the impacts of what we do. Continuing the assertiveness example, if we have a pattern of being aggressive a measure of success could be that we end discussions or negotiations still in respectful and good relations with others, whereas previously there was conflict. Or that others are now voicing alternatives to us, or maybe that the flow of people leaving our team is stemmed. It may be simpler, that we have repaired a damaged relationship with a colleague.

For context related goals we may need to rely on our own 'felt sense' of the change that we have made. If we are working on our values for example our measure of success could be that we feel that we have integrated and embodied them. Or, if we are deepening our level of self-awareness success would be reaching a good level of understanding of why we operate the way that we do under pressure, or perhaps of why we need to exert so much control.

Set a timeframe

Having deadlines helps us with focus. The timing is almost entirely ours unless others are applying pressure, and the choice whether to state three or six months, or something shorter or longer, is based on how hard or easy the goal might be to reach and how important it is to us and those around us.

It may take us two weeks to get clear about what we stand for, and a year to fully integrate it into our leadership identity. The former is likely to be a single event, while the latter may require some interim milestones. For example, by three months I want to feel as if I completely identify with my values. By six months I want them to have influenced my approach in one or two practical decisions. By nine months I will have reflected deeply on whether how I live and work is compatible with my values. By twelve months I will feel that my values are fully integrated and embodied.

Capture success
As we have seen personal change can be hard, and affirming our progress along the way will sustain us as we continue towards our goal. This may be a small win from our new skill, or feedback from a colleague, or that we have ticked off a milestone. Anyone that has climbed up a mountain or cycled up a long, steep hill knows that we keep fixated on the summit as we inch closer and closer. Just occasionally it can feel amazing to look back down into the valley and see how far we have come. We might be surprised by what we have already achieved, notwithstanding that there is still some

way to go.

Our 30-day habit building reflective practice is a great way to own and bank our successes.

Capturing success also requires a good attitude to the setbacks we may experience along the way. Our failures on the road to success are how we continue to learn. Remaining with a growth mindset will enable us to handle setbacks far more effectively than a fixed mindset.

Remind ourselves why we are doing this
Bringing to mind why we have elected to change something in the first place is energizing as we recall the realities of how we used to behave and operate. We might have forgotten this as we get stuck in the weeds of trying to do something differently, or if what we have tried to do has not yet worked for us as we had hoped. We may be stuck with half-formed neural pathways in our slightly clumsy stage of conscious competence. Keeping our eyes on the prize at the end of the road, while recalling whatever impulse it was that propelled us into development in the first place, will strengthen our resolve to keep working towards our goal. This may be as simple as the recollection that what got us here won't get us there, and it will be linked to our measure of success (2).

Get support
Managing our development is always far easier

when we have people in our corner. These could be people that have personal experience of what we are doing and can mentor us, people that simply want the best for us and will provide encouragement and a friendly word, and people that will ask us if we are doing what we said we would do. As you build your support team around you make sure you are clear what you want from them.

Once we have voiced our development goals to someone else we are likely to feel a sense of accountability to them for our commitments, far more so than if we kept them to ourselves. This sense of accountability will spur us on and provide energy.

Reflection as we know is an essential component of successful development and growth, and as we have already seen a great enabler as we work to embed learning and new skills, build new habits, and cultivate our wisdom. If necessary go back to chapter 3 to remind yourself of the power of the practice of reflection, in particular the 30-day habit builder.

"Nature loves courage. You make the commitment and nature will respond to that commitment by removing impossible obstacles. Dream the impossible dream and the world will not grind you under, it will lift you up. This is the trick. This is what all these teachers and philosophers who really counted, who really touched the alchemical gold, this is what they understood. This is the shamanic

dance in the waterfall. This is how magic is done. By hurling yourself into the abyss and discovering it's a feather bed."

- *Terence McKenna, Ethnobotanist*

SUMMARY

- Changing is hard for many reasons and perhaps none more so than the fear of letting go of safety. A change to the way that we operate can *appear* as threatening to our complex psychological identity even if it is what we need and something that we have initiated.

- Our *Hidden Competing Commitments* and our associated *Assumptions* unconsciously keep things just as they are.

- It is the stopping doing rather than the starting doing that is usually the most difficult.

- It can take many weeks of repetitive practice for us to complete the neural pathway rewiring that accompanies learning and development. Be aware that change is a process that takes time.

- There are proven hints and tips for increasing the probability of making change stick.

EXERCISES

1. Complete the Kegan template (with examples on the next page) to flush out your hidden competing commitments and your underlying assumptions with a development goal that you have. Take your time with this reflective work, and persevere. The insights may need encouragement to be teased out. Once you have done this see your hidden competing commitments and assumptions for what they are, and use the insights to manage a different conversation with yourself. Now, you can plan and follow through with your development actions despite your unconscious 'brakes', rather than being inhibited by them.

2. Each morning when you wake up, or whenever your 'day' starts, make a conscious choice to adopt a growth mindset for as much of your day as you are able. Make reminders to do this, a notice on a table, or a post-it on a fridge. Set a recurring diary entry for midday to remind you. Make use of the resources in note 35 for more information about growth vs. fixed mindset.

3. Work with the six proven tips for making change stick. These come from decades of coaching practice by countless coaches. The importance of having a

goal that you can fully commit to cannot be overstated in enabling you to achieve what you want to.

1. My visible commitment	2. What I do / don't do that stops me reaching my goal	3. My hidden commitment(s)	4. My big assumptions
(What I want to achieve)	(What I do when I get in my own way)	(What I say to myself that makes me do what I do when I get in my own way)	(What I am trying to avoid by making my hidden commitments)
My goal is to manage my boundaries better so that I don't get overwhelmed	I say yes even when I don't have capacity to take any more on	I am committed to fitting in and belonging to my work group	If I push back and say no others will reject me
	I don't push back when other people criticise me	I am committed to not rocking the boat	If I manage my boundaries others will not like me
	I work through all of my breaks and long after others have left	I am committed to working until all of my tasks are done	If I prioritise my needs, I will get a reputation for being difficult
	I don't stand up for myself	I am committed to other people's needs being met ahead of my own	If I stand up for myself I will be punished
		I am committed to avoiding conflict	If I get into conflict, I won't be able to control myself, and I will get into trouble
		I am committed to pushing myself as it is the only way to get on	If I don't push myself, I will get left behind

Examples in italics

TEN

INTEGRATION

"Dear Overripe Avocado, thank you for reminding me there is such a thing as waiting too long to be ready."
- *Andrea Gibson, via Instagram*

We now know that throughout our entire lives we continue to mature, change, develop, and grow, forever peeling back more and more interesting layers of who we are to reveal ever greater depth and capacity. I hope that by now you have accepted the invitation to grow and develop, to become the best version of yourself that you can possibly be right now, knowing that there is always more to come as the journey continues.

We have looked at how the ebbs and flows of our everyday lives present us with what we need to learn, if we pay enough attention. We have explored how to build our self-awareness and develop a mindful and curious attitude, and learned about the power of personal reflection for our change agency. We have dived deeply into different aspects of our psychological and emotional identity, the two huge engines that drive our behaviour, and understood how we can use fresh and revealing personal insights to accelerate our growth. We know where we have come from and how we have been shaped, and have defined what we stand for. We are far clearer as a result. We have discovered how to cultivate and use our innate wisdom. Finally, we have acknowledged the harsh reality that getting change to stick can be difficult, and taken on some ways of integrating and embodying what we have learned.

As we have worked through this book we will almost certainly have come to realise that each and every one of us is on a similar path, perhaps with just a little more or a little less experience than we have, and yet grappling with issues and challenges just as we do, even if it doesn't look like it from the outside.

Ultimately, we have learned what it is to be both individually and collectively minded, and to balance our needs with those of others so that together we can get done what we need and want to.

Well done! Look back and see how far the road travelled has been for you. If you are like most of us you will feel simultaneously the same and yet also different. *"The past is a foreign country; they do things differently there"* wrote L.P. Hartley in his novel The Go-Between. We will still speak the language and understand how they do things in the past, and will also know that we have developed a capacity that far exceeds what we could have done had we remained there.

This is why the development work is worth it.

By developing psychological and emotional maturity, and cultivating our wisdom, our life is increasingly lived on our own terms. We no longer 'act out' on others or seek out the drama, instead looking for how we can be a part of the solution to whatever problem we and others are facing. We see things for what they are. We have become the architect of who we are, and providing we remain curious and open-minded we can continue crafting our life right into old age. Our maturing enables us to be more genuinely connected with others, both at the individual as well as the societal level, because we will have thought deeply about how our work affects the people that we work with and the communities that we live in.

The decisions that we make now will be different as they take account of others needs in a far broader way than we used to, including the future generations. Our decisions will continue to be the right ones, and hopefully they will also be wise. Our leadership is now far more compelling, way more effective in a greater range of situations, and highly impactful.

In short, we can now achieve far more by doing less, as we use our next generation leadership skills.

The final task now that you have reached the end of this book is to consider how you will integrate what you have learned, and to work out what you want to focus on as your next development priority. The cycle of practice, reflection, and learning can continue for as long as you wish it to. My view is that to call a halt to this cycle is to begin a deterioration into a fixed old age, and to lose our 'juice' for living an enriched life. You may have a different view. From here on, for now, it is up to you.

ELEVEN

MY OWN EARLY LEADERSHIP STORY: WHY I WROTE THIS BOOK

This book began for me way back in the mists of time over thirty years ago, with a catastrophic career meltdown. It was catastrophic in the sense that it felt existential, profoundly threatening and deeply painful, as all personal crises must. With the kind of reflection and reframing that only the passage of time allows I now describe it as catalyzing, and in my most generous moods I can even bring myself to say it was a good thing. It was definitely a before and after moment, marking the time when my life would never be the same again.

I had managed to convince the company that I worked for that I had leadership potential, and with my one-eyed ambition and need for validation I happily accepted promotion to a level just that bit too far beyond my level of ability. I had potential for sure, and I still do and hope to until a ripe and healthy old age, however I had gaps in my experience that would come back to bite me, and hard.

Like a lot of people, I had been a successful

individual contributor promoted to management, and then after a while to managing and leading managers too. I received no training or mentoring, I was not offered any feedback, and had virtually no awareness of my strengths and where I needed to develop. It was purely a results business and I had delivered great results. My job was to just get others to do the same.

I enjoyed what I did well and turned a blind eye to what I didn't, and for quite a while this was more than enough. The results continued to accrue.

I wasn't however paying enough attention to what was changing around me. What I had been ignoring became more and more visible until I was faced with two equally important and competing objectives. They seemed to work against each other with my focus on one thing turning at the expense of the other. I had found myself in a leadership doom loop playing a zero-sum game.

I made some wrong calls and eventually it all came crashing down. The defining moment when things changed was when I had a directive right from the top to sack someone. I vividly remember meeting with Neil and Tony, his union rep. I don't know where it came from, when part way through it hit me with a startling clarity that this was simply the wrong thing to do. There was no proper evidence and it felt vindictive, and in that moment much to everyone's dismay I refused to follow it through and called a halt to the meeting, all the while knowing that it would be bad for my reputation and career.

My boss groaned when I told him, and the spotlight inevitably swung in my direction. From here it was only a matter of time and I was swiftly removed from my job and shunted sideways, where I could regroup and pick through the ruins. It was handled with a kind of brutal disdain; today we would describe the whole environment as toxic and bullying.

This was an exceptionally lonely phase. I felt wounded and diminished. My reputation was in shreds, my confidence was on the floor and my anxiety levels were through the roof. My relationship with power and authority was permanently changed, and in the process of failing I experienced a terrible shame and humiliation. My fragile ego had shattered.

Quite by chance I had not long before met someone outside of work who ended up fighting my corner. Judy was quite a bit older than me, with great skill and a refreshing, irreverent attitude. At last I no longer had to feel as if I was carrying such a heavy load all by myself, and with her support I weathered the immediate storm and then slowly began the long journey out of the fog and into working out where to go and what to do next.

With her help I began to see how lost and adrift I had become. I had little sense of who I was and had over-adapted to fit into what I imagined others expected of me. *"Whose life are you living?"* asks James Hollis, Jungian psychoanalyst [36], and all I knew at the time was that it wasn't mine.

To cope with the inherent insecurity that bubbles up from not living my own life, of not being true to who I was, I had developed ego-boosting behaviours and as a result had become emotionally disconnected, self-serving, and even arrogant. I did not like myself too much, I certainly did not enjoy my work, and I had no way to make any sense of what was going on.

With Judy's patient support I was encouraged to accept the harsh reality of what I was going through and to see it as something from which I could emerge stronger and happier, if a bit bruised. The questions that I began to ask myself then are what this book answers. Questions such as how had I become so adrift? Who actually am I and what does this mean for my work? How could I get to know myself better so that I could live a rich and satisfying life? What do I need to change in how I behave? If I discovered a personal red line by refusing to sack someone, what other red lines might I have? How does my work benefit those around me and perhaps even contribute to the society I live in?

Over time these questions and my search for answers became more important than any actual answers themselves. The discovery and teasing out of myself the information that I was after became a quest. And, it turns out, so began my professional journey that continues to this day.

I switched careers into learning and development, studying and practicing until many years later I found myself back in a leadership role, this time in professional services specialising in leadership development.

The initial post-catastrophe phase, what I came to call my "unlearning", of slowly acquiring self-awareness, of working out what to let go of, of figuring out what kind of person I wanted to be, took quite a while. It was only once I had stopped doing what wasn't serving me well that I was able to start the rebuilding process.

When I see it from a growth perspective then of course the catastrophe served me well. It was the single most important pivot in my life and a moment that has helped me to define who I am.

James Hollis describes vocation as where soul is added to job and duty, with the Latin derivative *vocatus* meaning "to be called". My work is what I love to do and after so long I think, and more importantly my clients think I am pretty good at it. Many of us end up teaching what we need to learn, and in the ongoing act of the learning we hopefully become better teachers. I am happy to allow myself to think that I have learned well.

ACKNOWLEDGEMENTS

There are many people involved in the creation of a book. I am enormously grateful to so many for their encouragement and support, especially when I got lost in the weeds. To India for her amazing editing, proof reading and publishing support. To Anna Bianchi, William Bloom, and Fran Creffield, for advice and ideas about the art and practice of book writing. To Sarah Jane Williamson for her insights and perception. To www.writershour.com for the writing space. To all of my clients and colleagues over many years for helping me to hone my craft. To HCubed for a wonderful professional network, that provided so much learning. To John Stockley for the book cover design. And to Caroline, who always believes in what I do.

ABOUT THE AUTHOR

Phil has over 40 years' experience working with some of the world's biggest and best known organisations across all continents.

He has dedicated over 30 years to his own spiritual and transpersonal development, initially under the supervision of the late Judy Fraser, and more latterly working with Dr. William Bloom. He is a leadership development expert, an educator, and a pioneer and original thinker at the intersection of where the mainstream and the alternative worlds meet.

With wisdom, curiosity, and humility, he believes more than ever in the transformative power of relationships; with ourselves, with others, and with community and society. He has enormous skill and a long track record in helping men and women of all ages connect with the very best of themselves. Above all else, he works with an attitude of love, service, and compassion.

He currently works as an educator in a spiritual health and wellbeing charity. He is also a trustee at The Chalice Well, world peace garden in Glastonbury.

BIBLIOGRAPHY

1. *The Leadership Pipeline*, Charan, Drotter, and Noel. Published by Jossey-Bass.

2. *The Chimp Paradox*, Dr Steve Peters. Published by Vermilion.

3. Carl Jung, C.W. Vol. 11: *Psychology and Religion: West and East.*

4. https://en.wikipedia.org/wiki/Subject_(philosophy)#:~:text=A%20subject%20is%20a%20being,object%20is%20a%20thing%20observed.

5. *Three Stages of Moral Development*. Lawrence Kohlberg. 1958.

6. www.harthill.co.uk

7. www.integrallife.com

8. https://www.researchgate.net/publication/356357233_Ego_Development_A_Full-Spectrum_Theory_Of_Vertical_Growth_And_Meaning_Making

9. https://static1.squarespace.com/static/56d2aa3720c647cdb3fe6dfb/t/5babdaa324a6941f39ac8c4d/1537989283963/Brown_2012_Leading+complex+change+with+post-conventional+consciousness.pdf

10. *Authentic Business: How to Create and Run Your Perfect Business,* Neil Crofts. 2005. Published by John Wiley & Sons.

11. https://www.16personalities.com/free-personality-test

    https://www.shl.com/shldirect/en/practice-tests/

    https://hrsoul.com/free-lumina-spark-personality-assessment/

    https://www.thepersonalitylab.org/home-2?gclid=CjwKCAjw4ZWkBhA4EiwAVJXwqb9DkcLNosrf0aM6-5MxYs16-JAOy-QysmE6Me4qr2e8jUWJ1TUvjBoCL5cQAvD_BwE

12. https://www.harthill.co.uk/ldp-report

13. *TA Today: A New Introduction to Transactional Analysis,* Ian Stewart and Vann Joines. 2nd edition 2012. Published by Lifespace.

14. *A Little Book on the Human Shadow,* Robert Bly. 1988. Published by HarperOne.

15. *Underland*. Robert MacFarlane. 2019. Published by Penguin.

16. www.exploringtheshadow.co.uk

17. *Emotional Intelligence: Why it can Matter More than IQ,* Daniel Goleman. 1995. Published by Bantam.

18. https://www.sciencedirect.com/science/article/abs/pii/S0278262603002859

19. https://www.psychologytoday.com/gb/blog/hide-and-seek/201601/what-are-basic-emotions

20. https://www.ncbi.nlm.nih.gov/pmc/articles/PMC3004979/

21. *Getting to Yes.* Roger Fisher and William Ury. 2012. Published by Random House Business.

22. *The Effect of Criticism on Functional Brain Connectivity and Associations with Neuroticism.* Michelle Servaas et al. Published July 26 2013.

23. *The Advantage.* Patrick Lencioni. 2012. Published by Jossey-Bass

24. *Discover Your True North.* Bill George. 2015. Published by Jossey-Bass.

25. *Character Strengths and Virtues: A Handbook and Classification.* Christopher Peterson and

Martin Seligman. 2004. Published by OUP USA.

26. *The Essentials of Theory U.* C. Otto Scharmer. 2018. Published by Berrett-Koehler.

27. *An Introduction to Johari Window.* Dinesh Soni. 2019. Published by Kindle.

28. https://healthyaging.ucsd.edu/research/sd-wise.html

29. *The Undiscovered Self.* Carl Jung. 1957. Published by Routledge.

30. *The Leader as Martial Artist.* Arnold Mindell. 2014. Published by Deep Democracy Exchange.

31. *Immunity to Change.* Robert Kegan and Lisa Laskow Lahey. 2009. Published by Harvard Business Review.

32. *Experiences of Habit Formation: A Qualitative Study.* Lally, Wardle and Gardner. 2011. Published Psychology, Health and Medicine Vol. 16, No 4, august 2011, 484-489

33. *What is Neuroplasticity? A Psychologist Explains.* 2018. Published in PsychologyToday.com.

34. *The Four Stages of Competence.* Broadwell, Curtis and Warren. 1960. First referenced in textbook Management of Training Programs

at NYU.

35. *Mindset.* Carol Dweck. 2017 (revised edition). Published by Robinson.

36. *Finding Meaning in the Second Half of Life.* James Hollis. Published by Avery.